Meet the Author Behind The Best Test Prep for the GRE Computer Science Test

The best minds to help you get the best GRE scores

In this book, you'll find our commitment to excellence, an enthusiasm for the subject matter, and an unrivaled ability to help you master the GRE Computer Science Test. REA's dedication to excellence and our passion for education make this book the very best test prep for the GRE Computer Science Test.

Benjamin Wells, Ph.D., is currently a professor at the University of San Francisco where he teaches computer science and mathematics. He also serves as Faculty Scholar at the Lawrence Livermore National Laboratory, and is a Visiting Scholar at the University of California's Department of Mathematics in Berkeley.

As one of the last students to study under the famed logician Alfred Tarski, Dr. Wells focuses his mathematical and scientific expertise on the academic boundaries shared by algebra, logic, and computing. His additional areas of research include hypercomputation, computer graphics, and historical computers. For the past decade, Dr. Wells has directed the Graduate Computer Science Program at the University of San Francisco, where he advises and coaches students interested in taking the GRE Computer Science Test.

The Best Test Preparation for the

GRE® 5th Edition

Computer Science Test

Benjamin Wells, Ph.D.
Computer Science and Mathematics Professor
University of San Francisco
San Francisco, CA

Research & Education Association
61 Ethel Road West
Piscataway, New Jersey 08854

THE BEST TEST PREPARATION FOR THE
GRE® COMPUTER SCIENCE SUBJECT TEST

Printed in the United States of America

Library of Congress Control Number 2005927682

International Standard Book Number 0-87891-434-X

REA® is a registered trademark of Research & Education Association, Inc.,
Piscataway, New Jersey 08854.

E05

CONTENTS

Chapter 1: Test-Taking Tools   1

Chapter 2: During the Exam   19

Chapter 3: Content Discussion and Review   29

Chapter 4: More Specialized Knowledge   67

Chapter 5: Practice Test   77

About Research & Education Association

Founded in 1959, Research & Education Association is dedicated to publishing the finest and most effective educational materials—including software, study guides, and test preps—for students in middle school, high school, college, graduate school, and beyond.

REA's Test Preparation series includes books and software for all academic levels in almost all disciplines. Research & Education Association publishes test preps for students who have not yet entered high school, as well as high school students preparing to enter college. Students from countries around the world seeking to attend college in the United States will find the assistance they need in REA's publications. For college students seeking advanced degrees, REA publishes test preps for many major graduate school admission examinations in a wide variety of disciplines, including engineering, law, and medicine. Students at every level, in every field, with every ambition can find what they are looking for among REA's publications.

REA's practice tests are always based upon the most recently administered exams, and include every type of question that you can expect on the actual exams.

REA's publications and educational materials are highly regarded and continually receive an unprecedented amount of praise from professionals, instructors, librarians, parents, and students. Our authors are as diverse as the fields represented in the books we publish. They are well-known in their respective disciplines and serve on the faculties of prestigious high schools, colleges, and universities throughout the United States and Canada.

Today, REA's wide-ranging catalog is a leading resource for teachers, students, and professionals.

We invite you to visit us at *www.rea.com* to find out how "REA is making the world smarter."

Staff Acknowledgments

In addition to Dr. Wells, we would like to thank REA's Larry B. Kling, Vice President, Editorial, for supervising development; Pam Weston, Vice President, Publishing, for setting the quality standards for production integrity and managing the publication to completion; Stacey Farkas, Senior Editor, for coordinating development; Diane Goldschmidt, Associate Editor, for post-production quality assurance; Gianfranco Origliato for his editorial contributions; Reena Shah for technical editing; Jeff LoBalbo, Senior Graphic Artist, for interior page design; and Christine Saul, Senior Graphic Artist, for cover design. We also thank Michael Cote for page composition.

This book would not have been possible without the contributions of the following: Gregory D. Benson, Ph.D., Jeff T. Buckwater, Ph.D., Jean-Claude Franchitti, Ph.D., Hang Lau, Ph.D., Baekjun Lim, M.S., and Randall Raus, M.S.

About the Book

This book provides an accurate and complete representation of the Graduate Record Examination in Computer Science. Our full-length practice test is based on the format of the current GRE Computer Science Subject Test. The test is 170 minutes in length and includes every type of question that can be expected on the actual exam. Following our test is an answer key, complete with detailed explanations designed to clarify the material for you. By completing the practice test and studying the explanations that follow, you'll be able to pinpoint your strengths and weaknesses and thereby become well-prepared for the actual test.

About the Test

The GRE Computer Science Subject Test is offered twice a year by the Educational Testing Service under the direction of the Graduate Record Examinations Board. Applicants for graduate school submit GRE test results together with other academic records as part of the highly competitive admission process. The GRE Subject Tests are intended to provide the graduate school admissions committee with a means of evaluating students' competence in certain subject areas.

The questions on the test are composed by experts in the field of computer science who teach at various undergraduate and graduate institutions throughout the United States. The questions are designed to determine students' understanding of computer science concepts, as well as their ability to apply these concepts to specific situations.

The test consists of approximately 70 multiple-choice questions. Some questions are grouped together and refer to a particular diagram, graph, or program fragment. Emphasis is placed on the following major areas of computer science. The given percentages are approximate because these proportions may differ from administration to administration.

Software Systems and Methodology (40%)
- Organization of Data
- Program Control and Structure
- Languages and Notation
- Software Engineering
- Systems

Computer Organization and Architecture (15%)
- Processors/Control Units
- I/O Devices
- High-Performance Architectures
- Logic Design
- Memories

Theory and Mathematics (40%)
- Algorithm Analysis
- Automata and Language Theory
- Discrete Structures

Special Topics (5%)
- Typical topics may include artificial intelligence, graphics, simulation and modeling, and data communication.

Scoring the Test

After taking the sample test, check your answers against the solution key provided at the end of the test. Each correct answer receives one "raw score" point, each incorrect answer deducts $\frac{1}{4}$ of a point, and any omissions should not be counted. Round the resulting total to the nearest whole number. This number represents your total raw score. Use the formula below to help you calculate your raw score.

$$\underset{\substack{\text{number} \\ \text{right}}}{\_\_\_\_\_} - (\underset{\substack{\text{number} \\ \text{wrong}^*}}{\_\_\_\_\_} \times \tfrac{1}{4}) = \underset{\substack{\text{raw} \\ \text{score}}}{\_\_\_\_\_} \quad \text{(round to nearest whole number)}$$

Then, use the given table to convert your raw score from the practice test into a scaled score. This enables you to compare your performance with that of other students.

*Do not include unanswered questions

Scaled Score Conversions
for REA's GRE Computer Science Practice Test

TOTAL SCORE			
Raw Score	Scaled Score	Raw Score	Scaled Score
70	910	36-37	690
68-69	900	35	680
		33-34	670
67	890	32	660
65-66	880	30-31	650
64	870	29	640
62-63	860	27-28	630
61	850	26	620
59-60	840	24-25	610
57-58	830	22-23	600
55-56	820		
54	810	21	590
53	800	19-20	580
		18	570
51-52	790	16-17	560
50	780	15	550
48-49	770	13-14	540
47	760	12	530
46	750	10-11	520
44-45	740	9	510
42-43	730	7-8	500
41	720		
39-40	710	6	490
38	700	4-5	480
		2-3	470
		1	460
		0	450

*This table is provided for scoring only REA's practice test for the GRE Computer Science Subject Test. Candidates interested in scoring for a particular GRE test form should visit the GRE Website *www.gre.org*. The site provides information on percentile ranking.

Helpful Hints

While taking the practice test, it is helpful to observe the same conditions that will be encountered during the actual test administration.

- Work in a quiet place, free from distractions and interruptions.

- Do not use any reference materials, since these items are not allowed for use during the test.

- Work straight through the test. Extra time and short breaks do not occur during the actual exam.

- Time yourself accurately, if possible with a watch or clock alarm. Looking up to check the time will act as a distraction. (But note that watches with alarms are not permitted at the testing center.)

- Since incorrect answers are penalized $\frac{1}{4}$ of a point each, and unanswered questions are not counted, it is not a good idea to guess. However, if you are able to eliminate one or more of the answers, guessing may be to your advantage statistically (that is, the odds of choosing the right answer improve).

Notations & Conventions

Notations and Conventions

In this test a reading knowledge of programming languages is assumed. The following notational conventions are used on the test.

1. All numbers are assumed to be written in decimal notation unless otherwise indicated.

2. $\lfloor x \rfloor$ denotes the greatest integer that is less than or equal to x.

3. $\lfloor x \rfloor$ denotes the least integer that is greater than or equal to x.

4. $g(n) = O(f(n))$ denotes "$g(n)$ has order $f(n)$" and, for purposes of this

   test, may be taken to mean that $\lim_{x \to \infty} \left| \frac{g(n)}{f(n)} \right|$ is finite.

   $g(n) = \Omega(f(n))$ denotes "$g(n)$ has order at least $f(n)$" and for the purpose of this test means there exist positive constants C and N such that $g(n) \geq C_2 f(n)$ for all $n > N$.

   $g(n) = \Theta(f(n))$ denotes "$g(n)$ has the sane order as $f(n)$" and means that there exist positive constants C_1 and C_2, and N such that $C_1 f(n) \leq g(n) \leq C_2 f(n)$ for all $n > N$.

5. $\exists$ denotes "there exists."

   $\forall$ denotes "for all."

   $\Rightarrow$ denotes "implies."

   $\neg$ denotes "not"; "A" is also used as meaning "$\neg A$."

   $\vee$ denotes "inclusive or."

   $\oplus$ denotes "exclusive or."

$\wedge$ denotes "and"; also, juxtaposition of statements denotes "and," e.g., PQ denotes "P and Q."

A boolean formula is <u>satisfiable</u> if it is true under some assignment of boolean values for its variables.

A boolean formula is a <u>tautology</u> (or is <u>valid</u>) if it is true under all assignments of boolean values for its variables.

6. $\emptyset$ denotes the empty set.

If A and B denote sets, then:

$A \cup B$ is the set of all elements that are in A or in B or in both;

$A \cap B$ is the set of all elements that are in both A and B; AB also denotes $A \cap B$;

$\overline{A}$ is the set of all elements not in A that are in some specified universal set.

$|A|$ is the cardinality of A.

7. In a string expression, if S and T denote strings or sets of strings, then:

An empty string is denoted by ε or by Λ;

ST denotes the concatenation of S and T;

$S + T$ denotes

$S \cup T$ or $\{S, T\}$ depending on context;

S^n denotes $\underbrace{SS...S}_{n \text{ factors}}$;

$S*$ denotes $\varepsilon + S + S^2 + S^3 + ...$;

S^+ denotes $S + S^2 + S^3 + ...$

8. In a grammar:

$\alpha \rightarrow \beta$ represents α production in the grammar.

$\alpha \Rightarrow \beta$ means β can be derived from α by the application of exactly one production.

$\alpha \stackrel{*}{\Rightarrow} \beta$ means β can be derived from α by the application of zero or more productions.

Unless otherwise specified

   (i)   symbols appearing on the left-hand side of productions are nonterminal symbols, the remaining symbols are terminal symbols,

   (ii) the leftmost symbol of the first production is the start symbol,

   (iii) the start symbol is permitted to appear on the right-hand side of productions.

9.   In a logic diagram:

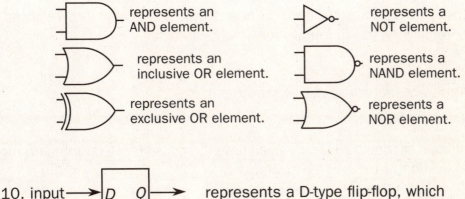

   represents an AND element.

   represents a NOT element.

   represents an inclusive OR element.

   represents a NAND element.

   represents an exclusive OR element.

   represents a NOR element.

10. input $\longrightarrow$ D   Q $\longrightarrow$

    clock $\longrightarrow$ > $\overline{Q}$ $\longrightarrow$

    represents a D-type flip-flop, which stores the value of its D input when clocked.

11. Binary tree traversal is defined recursively as follows:

     preorder — visit the root, traverse the left subtree, traverse the right subtree inorder — traverse the left subtree, visit the root, traverse the right subtree

postorder — traverse the left subtree, traverse the right subtree, visit the root

12. In a finite automaton diagram, states are represented by circles, with final (or accepting) states indicated by two concentric circles. The start state is indicated by the word "Start." An arc from state s to state t labeled a indicates a transition from s to t on input a. A label a / b indicates that this transition produces an output b. A label $a_1, a_2, ..., a_k$ indicates that the transition is made on any of the inputs $a_1, a_2, ..., a_k$.

13. For a program segment S and predicates P and Q, to say that triple $\{P\}S\{Q\}$ is partially correct means that if P is true before initiaton of S, then Q is true upon the termination of S. To say that $\{P\}S\{Q\}$ is totally correct means that it is partially correct and S teminates for all imputs for which P is true

14. A loop variant for a `while` statement

        while B do S

    is an assertion that is true each time the guard B is evaluated during execution of the `while` statement.

Chapter 1
Test-Taking Tools

Test-Taking Tools

Before the Exam

How will this book benefit me?

- You're taking the GRE Computer Science Subject test cold, so reviewing the most relevant material and trying practice exams will acquaint you with the required tasks of exam day. In the process, you'll build confidence and allay anxiety.

- You have taken the GRE/CS before, but you are retaking it because you want to improve your score; now you need to focus on problems that you recall giving you trouble—the ones whose tough answer choices precluded you from making a reasonable guess, the ones that took too much time to reach the certainty of a correct answer, and the ones that simply baffled you.

- You took the GRE/CS five years ago, and now the Educational Testing Service will not report your score, so you are retaking it with five years' experience but the same interval beyond the classroom; therefore, you need to reorient yourself with test-taking and with the scope and topics specific to the GRE/CS.

Review materials

How do you study for the GRE Subject Test in Computer Science (GRE/CS)? Some wisdom gathered from the personal experiences of students and faculty members will be presented, but in the end, it remains a more difficult exam to study for and to take than the GRE General Test and other similar general knowledge examinations. Indeed, some experts hold that it is too content-specific to be approached with general test-taking strategies. By contrast, our position is that content review, skill sharpening, and testing stratgey are available, feasible, and beneficial.

Is there a book that helps? We believe this one does, but the questioner usually also wants guidance to appropriate computer science texts. At the elementary level, it will be helpful to look through a text for what some call the bridge course. This course, perhaps less popular now, assumes familiarity with computers and elementary computer science, but does not presume any depth of knowledge. It is typically taught after the first programming course or set of courses and before the first of the upper-level classes or advanced lower-level courses (for example, before a course in algorithms or architecture). A good choice here is the latest edition of Brookshear's *Computer Science: An Overview.*

Reading such a book will show you whether there are major gaps in your preparation. It will benefit you to read (and work problems or write programs) in those sections. This will not be the equivalent of a focused text or course, but it is likely that only a few questions on the GRE/CS would be covered by that material anyway. It will also give you a general review of the scope of the GRE/CS.

The next level of useful texts are those typically adopted for core undergraduate courses. If some time has passed since you took the course, it will help to review your text or a similar one. Recall that no course covers all the material in its texts, and the GRE/CS respects that tendency by sticking to the main and common concepts in any particular area. So you should focus on the first few chapters and those that are indicated by the authors of the texts in their own introductions as being appropriate for the usual undergraduate course. Students rarely note that most texts tell the instructor which parts are commonly taught. For example, Lewis and Papadimitriou's *Elements of the Theory of Computation* 2e, the first 3–5 sections of each of the first 3–4 chapters are the essential core.

I will not recommend a text per course because you are already familiar with one particular text that will seem amazingly useful when you return to it for review, simply because you have covered much ground with it already. In other words, a certain text that I view as very poor for teaching discrete math will find supporters among many students, simply because that is the one they know best.

In fact, for each field, it may help to compare several texts, ignoring the topics peculiar to any single book. Beware of texts that do not provide standard coverage of material. For example, most automata texts start with finite state machines, but at least one starts with primitive recursive functions—will *those teachers* get to what the exam covers? Be more cautious of books that are true outliers, such as the title that superficially appears to be an automata book, but in fact is an exposition of a research area, that has little in common with the usual content.

There are several tailored study guides for the GRE/CS listed online, including an outdated edition of this one. I recommend that you read the online reviews of these, as well as reviews of any texts or surveys you are contemplating buying (don't forget to check with your libraries first).

You will also find that review summaries—like REA's *Essentials of Computer Science*—will be helpful in retracing your own learning, supplementing it in weaker areas, or calling your attention to topics that you must spend a moderate amount of time studying.

The only review guide that you should buy (assuming you have your own copy of this book) is one published by the Educational Testing Service—*GRE: Practicing to Take the Computer Science Test* (referred to below as *ETS/CS*), which has the advantage of containing an actual discontinued GRE/CS exam as well as additional practice problems; the disadvantage is that no solutions beyond an answer key are provided. Three editions exist; all are out of print, but you can still find used copies. Each contains a released exam, from 1986, 1991, and 1996.

Currently, ETS supplies a hardcopy practice book to every GRE/CS test registrant, and the same document is available for download in Adobe PDF format. This fifty-five page booklet contains two-pages of useful test-taking advice plus an actual exam from 2003. It does not contain the additional practice problems all editions of ETS/CS and an older free booklet featured. It has an answer key, but offers no solutions or explanations. Download it at:

ftp://ftp.ets.org/pub/gre/CompSci.pdf

The percent chart for topic coverage included at the beginning of this book is an approximation to the approximation given by ETS. For the real thing, consult:

http://www.gre.org/subdesc.html#compsci

or, better, the free practice book, which also contains this information.

Of course, the main reason to look online is to discover excellent tutorials on every aspect of computer science, including those very topics in which you are weak. Usually these are posted by instructors or research groups. Newsgroups and chat facilities can provide answers, either from archives or in near-realtime. Typically useful sites include these four:

1. The Free Online Dictionary of Computing is ideal for general information, providing over 13,000 entries:

   http://nightflight.com/foldoc/

2. BABEL, providing a list of 5,000 acronyms and abbreviations, can be found at:

   http://www.geocities.com/ikind_babel/babel/babel.html

3. The NIST Dictionary of Algorithms, Data Structures, and Problems, is a specialized resource that includes nearly 1,400 entries:

   http://www.nist.gov/dads/

4. The Jargon File or Jargon Dictionary, is an excellent resource when one encounters obscure and unfamiliar terminology or phrases. It has 2,300 entries in v.4.4.7; check it at:

   http://catb.org/~esr/jargon/

   or a browser-friendly version of v4.2.2 at:

   http://info.astrian.net/jargon/

Please understand that these are merely examples; they have been selected for the likelihood of their reliable accessibility or for their relevance. We cannot guarantee that you will find them or any documents mentioned below at the cited URLs, but there will always be a wealth of information on the Web.

Your library or professional organization may offer online resources, too. Topping the list is the Association for Computing Machinery's http://portal.acm.org/, which for student members costs less per year than most CS books. It is possible that your library may offer this and other such subscription databases without charge to on-campus or proxy-server users, so check with your reference librarian for access rules and methods.

Problem solving

Why should you focus on solving problems? For one thing, it's because questions on the GRE/CS come in three sorts: recognizing and applying definitions, using concepts, and solving problems of one or more layers. Although there will be scant opportunity to demonstrate your knowledge of basic/elementary CS facts (think of the proverbial dates in a history course), there will be a few questions that involve little more than recognizing the fact within the language. More frequently, you must apply a concept to identify the correct scope of a proposed solution or characterization. Most readers, however, would count most of the test's items (questions) as problems. Some may require you to do no more than take the given information and draw a conclusion; let's call this a one-layer problem. Other questions will involve intermediate solutions leading in a chain to the final answer. We should also include in this group most of the questions that offer alternatives of this form:

A.　　I and II only
B.　　III only

and so forth. Because these inevitably require several correct solutions of distinct one-layer problems, they are really equivalent to multilayer problems.

We now turn to the issue of practice problems in general. Experience has shown that working problems is the best way to prepare for the GRE/CS. Of course, practice exams are required, but one must go beyond multiple-choice questions of this sort. First, you need to have confidence in solving problems for which no list of solutions is proposed; then you will be better prepared to approach alternatives listed on the exam problems. Let us distinguish three kinds of problems: content-based, skills-based, and mathematical. These are not disjoint categories. But they are distinct from the earlier categorization into three levels of difficulty; here, we deal only with the third level, real problems.

Content problems require factual knowledge of a particular topic, such as, "Is the following grammar context free?" Skill-based problems may superficially require background, but more careful reading shows that your ability to apply CS principles, not facts, in a novel situation is what is tested; an example is: "In the long-dead programming language Trojan the type of the variable Yellow at the position noted is charstring. Which of the following scoping methods could Trojan be using?" In addition, that yield to general test-taking methods should be grouped here.

Many problems can be approached as math tasks, even when at first glance they appear to be content- or skill-based.

How should one study for these three types of problems? Content problems are best practiced by doing the first few exercises in the homework sections of texts. Skills problems are likely to be in the subsequent, more difficult subsections. The math practice needs a few more words. You have taken five to nine courses that could be said to fall in the category of mathematics, but you may have not taken a course that required both mathematical rigor and mature mathematical reasoning. This is typically an outcome of the differences between the disciplines of mathematics and computer science; it is surely not a fault of your education. If you have math minor or double major, you will appreciate those differences.

So let us assume a level of mathematical sophistication briefly. You should try the more difficult problems in more theoretical subjects to whet your ability: algorithms, discrete structures, and automata in particular. The contention is that the particular topic does not matter as much as the attitude you have when you tackle an unfamiliar problem with a toolkit of standard mathematical techniques. This approach can help you with skills-based problems when you lack the immediate context of their content. Typical problems on the GRE/CS that yield to this are scheduling problems in resource allocation that may be trivial for a student who is familiar with the particular content, but can easily be solved in perhaps twice the time by mathematical methods, regardless of the novelty of the subject matter.

Let us return to the reader who has had no sophisticated math training—how can he or she benefit from the mathematical approach, short of succeeding in a "professional" math course? Try this: attempt the harder problems as above, but seek the aid of someone with math skills who can help you rehearse the solutions once you attempt the problems. This will give you confidence and enhance your own considerable mathematical experience.

Do not underestimate the importance of this. I contend that students scoring near 900 have both strong factual knowledge and quick mathematical insight. Moreover, if your goal is to move from 500 to 600 or from 700 to 800, numerous problems can be solved quickly enough by viewing them as math problems—even if at first glance they appear to be wholly content based. This advice will do little good if you have not taken pains to practice the math.

Content review is straightforward, and tips on studying it wisely and efficiently will be offered in this guide. Math preparation

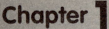

may be lengthy and not accessible to everyone (but recall that math problems in the usual sense will form 15% of your GRE/CS, and mathematically intense theory problems are another 25%). Despite the competitive edge that math gives, it is a skill that must be built. When it is, many problems of the other two types become more accessible. In other words, in the economy of test preparation, it is most beneficial to spend time in this area.

Skill acquisition

Some specialized skills will be best learned in classrooms and from working the textbook problems. More about that later. We turn here to the general skills. Begin by reading intelligently; skip historical notes and sidebars, and stick to reading top down: major concepts, then refinements and applications. Take notes. Outlines may be sketched at this point; they will be essential later. Practice the tasks of identification, comparison, and extension by finding the five most significant aspects of a topic, using these to associate it with similar topics, and then extract a common conceptual skeleton. This will help you classify problems on the exam quickly.

From the start of your review, practice confidence and relaxation. The first will keep you moving on through the challenges of unfamiliar material posed on the exam; the second will help you bring your best effort to the problems. Think of it as hiking uphill: you need to keep moving at a steady pace, but not get out of breath. Another quality to develop is imagination. During review, try novel problems, but also try novel attacks on standard problems. On the exam, your intuition may speak to you of a better approach or a clever trap, but without prior cultivation your sense of wonder and insight may not respond.

What about commercial courses in test-taking? There are still none intended for the GRE/CS; companies in the test-taking business say that the exam is too content based. We disagree because we have the impression that even on the Subject Tests, there are effective gains to be made from improving standard test-taking skills. Therefore, we suggest considering taking a course intended, say, for the GRE/General; or at least read a book or use related software. Besides, you may wish to retake that exam. Surprising as it may sound, another option is LSAT preparation, because the exam focuses on multilayer reasoning.

Students find that one of the best sources of assistance on the GRE/CS is a study group, of three to five colleagues. Unlike a team project, all team members learn everything, but there are some tasks that decompose and parallelize, such as gathering books, selecting topics for review, and preparing review presentations. Probably the greatest advantage is working with students who are strong in your weak areas. But the real selling point is having a support group before and even *after* the exam.

Calculation

The ability to calculate must be strongly emphasized. It is the quickest way to save time if you are proficient and the surest way to make errors if you are not. No calculators or other aids are allowed in the exam room (that is, they must be safely stowed in your carry-on beneath your seat before the exam takes flight). Although you will not be asked to multiply four-digit numbers, you will encounter numerous tasks of binary arithmetic, Boolean expressions, propositional calculus, and decimal estimation.

Practice tests

Now to the issue of practice tests. Our advice is simple; take them! There are four sample GRE/CS exams released by ETS, plus three out-of-print editions of ETS/CS with additional practice problem sets. The older exams are less relevant, but all are retired and students constantly complain that the real exam does not resemble the any of the published ones. Get serious! They are still completely useful apart from a few content-based questions. The exam in this book is intended to be more up-to-date than ETS/CS, but every GRE/CS is built from a question pool, of which a single exam represents but one sampling. One recent exam, for example, seemed to be downplaying automata and introducing more questions on WWW. Test-takers often have impressions of topic frequencies that vary from the real ones. There was a disturbing trend, however, that emerged in the recent exams. When I took the exam in fall 2002, I counted questions carefully. There were many more content-based questions, and I found the following skewing of the published percent distribution: 20% on trees and graphs, 10% on cache and virtual memory, and another 20% on RISC, parallel, hashing, netwokring, and P/NP. The highest predictable from ETS's Content chart for these topics is 27%. Although the released 2003 exam may still have some skewing, we cannot tell the pattern of the new exam until we see it.

With practice exams, allow yourself the luxury of doing at least one untimed. Force yourself to do at least two with the clock. During timed practice, try to follow the suggestions below for exam-day behavior.

The format of the response choices, or alternatives, is worth a few words. There are always five. Occasionally, the last is "None of the above," which makes exhaustive rejection of the first four options feasible, but hinders reverse engineering and guessing based on getting a trial answer close to an alternate answer (in problems where *close* makes sense, such as numeric ones). But the worst aspect is that it sabotages a strategy of spotting the most likely answer from the list of choices, an informal style of working backwards. If you are inclined to choose distractors (superficially attractive but incorrect alternatives), then you should avoid that strategy anyway. Note that "All of the above" is never an alternative, and any practice tests that use it are ill-constructed and probably not useful. Of course, the strongest indicator of a poor question is having "None of the above" as the fourth alternative and "All of the above" as the last. The fact that every question has a unique answer (and not "best answer" as on the LSAT) has been exploited to build exam puzzles (problems too tricky to appear on an actual exam), some quite ingenious. In the discussion of logic content that follows, there is a simple puzzle based on this constraint.

Concept questions are frequently asked, independent of any particular pedagogy, program, or technology. In the past, this meant asking only common core questions and sticking to standards, such as properties of Standard Pascal. The newer approach is to spend several paragraphs setting up a possibly unfamiliar (probably novel) technical situation, then asking one or more questions about it. This means that memorizing books will do little good, but it also means that seeing several related situations can help. So reading those books is required.

This is not the only type of clustered questioning. A set of consecutive questions frequently depends on a code fragment, a diagram or graph printed and explained before the first question in the set. The set often has two questions, sometimes three.

The most despised type of problem is one in which several statements (typically three, numbered *I, II, III*) are given, and then the answer alternatives are conjunctions of these, such as "I only," "I and III only," etc. These are sometimes justified by saying that there are not five natural alternatives, so the required five have to be synthesized. Even if the reasoning is doubtful, questions of this form are common. Essentially three problems must be worked correctly, namely the conclusions for I–III, before the final answer can be approached. Because there are eight possible synthetic alternatives (including "None"), and only five are used, you can sometimes get information from the form of the ones listed. For example, perhaps "II" only occurs with "III," which you already know to be false; so you don't bother working II. Or you would guess that I is false, but then you find it occurs in every alternative that remains; if you are confident in the rejections, then you need not worry about settling I—it must be true. Nonetheless, it is usually efficient to assign an initial truth value to each of I–III before considering the conjunctive alternatives.

Final preparations

Now come the two great secrets of test taking: outlining and rest. Two or three days before the exam, complete a detailed outline of all the subject areas you have reviewed. This might run 20 to 50 pages; obviously, the larger the number, the more you have been outlining all along! On the day before the exam, reduce this first to five pages, and then to a single page. You have now built an index of your knowledge. Why do it? Because most of us will find that once we commit it to paper, there will be a corresponding model of the outline in our minds that we can call on during the exam. This is not memorization; it is more of a personal knowledge key. Two more steps are required. Reread these outlines, ending with the briefest summary. Then apply the second secret:

rest. Do something relaxing (but not under the influence) the evening before the exam, set the alarm, and get a good night's sleep, relying on your preparation to be appropriate and available. You may or may not wish to reread the two summary outlines just before the exam.

Other advice and views

Let's face facts. There is widespread dissatisfaction among computer scientists with the GRE/CS (and this is well known to ETS). This unhappiness takes two forms. First, there are claims and complaints that the exam does not reflect the typical undergraduate CS education. Second, there are assertions that it does not provide a meaningful predictor of graduate success. The difficulty is the broad variety of CS undergraduate programs on the one hand; on the other hand, the impression grows that a high score on the exam is not correlated with good grades, productive habits, or domain competency in CS graduate programs. But until a new exam cycle addresses these concerns adequately, or sufficiently many graduate programs drop the requirement of the GRE/CS for admission or other purposes, the reality, if not the utility, of the exam is likely to persist.

Chapter 2
During the Exam

During the Exam

Getting settled

Remember to bring the required photo identification and your registration ticket. It is bound to be frustrating to enter the exam room; there may be delays, absurd identification procedures, and rules you did not read about. You will be surrounded by both anxious and proudly confident people. Luckily, you won't have to be aware of them during the exam. The proctors will attempt to tell you where to sit. If the chair is broken, tell them you will take a different one. Make sure you have many No. 2 pencils, in case proctors have no extras or there is no sharpener. Most rooms will in fact have both. Food is still not allowed, but given the ubiquity of bottled water, ETS now permits it. Follow the directions given before the exam; it will put you in a mood to pay attention to the written instructions within the exam.

Although you are not on a classroom grading curve, it can sometimes seem like the room is filled with people thinking more clearly than you, busier than you, competing with you, racing against you. But you really have no idea whether one test-taker is working desperately on a CS problem you have already completed, or whether another test-taker is staring at a biology problem with a blank memory. The tension level may be palpable, but you can focus on your work by remembering that this is a test, not a contest.

Choosing the questions

From the top of the exam, you need to think in terms of reaching the bottom and having some time left to review flagged questions. Divide the length of the exam by the number of items to give a time limit on each problem. This is one way it has worked: $170/70 = 2.4$ minutes per problem. Unless you spot a diagram (a personal example is a time-dependent circuit) that signals a problem you can immediately abandon, you will need to read each question in order to determine what to do with it. The recent exams include more extensive explanations in the questions. Thus, questions depend less critically on prior content knowledge, but if you must read for understanding rather than identification, the problem will take three to five times longer to work. The other reason to read carefully is that some problems are made more difficult by precise statements that you may misread if hurried. These should not be styled as tricky questions, although that's a good characterization of the feeling you may get from them.

Read for triage. If the problem can be done immediately, do it without hesitation; if it should be left for later consideration, strike out any alternatives that you can immediately identify as wrong, flag it in the test booklet, and add it to a list of problem numbers at the back of the booklet for later consideration. Do not mark it on the answer sheet. If you think a minute or two of extra work will yield an answer, put a star by it on your revisit list. A small fraction of problems can simply be abandoned at this time—if you don't know anything about resolution, half adders, second normal form, or dynamic programming, then staring at the question and the answer choices probably won't help. On the other hand, if you cannot remember the key fact or association immediately, it may be worth revisiting later.

Choosing the answers

Distractors are false alternatives whose appeal is calculated to fit the problem well. It may be a content problem with an obvious answer, which turns out to be wrong on careful reading. The distractor may be an answer found with an incorrect method. It may be the correct answer off by one. In short, one should be guarded about all conveniently right answers. Conversely, the GRE/CS does not waste time with flippant or absurd answers. This means that an odd answer may deserve another look.

The form of the alternatives may help you discard some from the start; some may be clearly out of range, or otherwise inappropriate. Now let's try to find the right answer.

There are two ways of working a problem: top down and bottom up. In the former, work the problem without looking at the alternatives. If you feel that you carefully considered all the information in the problem and your solution is sound, then take the alternative that has your answer. Do not select an answer that is merely close to yours; if your answer is not there, rework the problem.

Working from the bottom up begins with the alternatives and reverse-engineers the problem. Sometimes checking answers is more efficient than working the original problem. Sometimes the route to a solution is suggested by a pattern in the alternatives, even if no answer jumps out as correct from the start. Distractors can contribute to the pattern, too.

With either method, confirmation should be sought— sometimes by working the problem both ways, sometimes by a second solution. What if the verification fails? Although it is easy to argue against it, generations of test-takers advise that once you answer a question, you should have a better than 60–70% confidence level to change it to something else. So even if your checking proves inconclusive, you should not abandon an answer without a strong sense that another is better.

Reviewing the doubtfuls

You have made one pass through the exam, and now you have a limited amount of time to review your flagged list, beginning with the starred problems first. Recompute the time per problem.

This is a good time to accept your own ignorance. If a problem seems too obscure or too convoluted, abandon it—any problem you skip is worth more than the one you miss.

Although finding the right answer is the ultimate goal, identifying wrong ones is certainly helpful along the way. ETS penalizes wrong answers (but not blank answers) by deducting one-fourth the number of wrong answers from the right answers to yield the "formula score." This removes any probabilistic benefit from guessing; but ETS advises guessing if at least one alternative can be discarded as wrong. We go further: guessing is mandatory if two or three alternatives are known to be wrong, and we advise guessing in any case where you feel there is a nonuniform distribution of "rightness" among the alternatives. Unless you have a hunch, informed or otherwise, you will maximize your guessing score by choosing from among the remaining choices randomly.

Despite this advice that favors guessing, we also urge you to leave blank those problems for which you have no hunch and no firm discards. Otherwise, you can become a sucker for an attractive distractor and a target for the wrong-answer penalty. Students have made disastrous mistakes by marking all problems. Yet despite study guides and exam instructions stating the contrary, some students believe false rumors that every question should be answered, while others are convinced that one should never guess. Both groups are deluded.

Using past experience

We have already mentioned the value of the published exams in the ETS/CS series. Despite some curious language on the ETS site, if a faculty member inquires for previous exams, he or she will be sent a free copy of the latest released exam. Unless one works for ETS, there is no other source of old exams. There may be bootleg debriefed versions from students who have taken the exam, but ETS extracts a promise from each test-taker to reveal no questions. Unfortunately, schemes for selling answers have been reported; some have resulted in criminal cases.

Nonetheless, hearsay can still be useful; nothing prevents examinees from sharing the topics covered, as well as those *not* covered. Can this actually be useful for other students? In other words, how much can a few sample tests predict what you will encounter on the exam? We know that about every five years, ETS discontinues and decommissions an exam cycle, and that the published sample exam represents that cycle.

Evidence for a single exam is given by the apparent success of a fraud that involved examiners capturing questions on the East Coast of the U.S., and selling answers to test-takers on the West Coast, who began the exam period three hours later.

How does this affect our discussion? There is no indication that exams given in different months are identical, although here is an argument that they are related. The scaled score is a strictly monotonically increasing function of the formula score with values ranging from 200 to 900. This function is designed to give the examinee a score that is comparable across different exam instances and cycles. We will not discuss the latter, for there seems to be some counterevidence concerning that. Now, also consider the percentile score, which gives the percent of examinees participating in each exam cycle scoring less than a particular scaled score. Whenever you ask ETS for an exam report on a particular exam date, you will always get the same scaled score (at least during the period in which they will report old scores). Now comes the crucial fact: over the course of the last decade or two, the percentiles have decreased as the exam cycle wears on. In other words, a scaled score of 700 may have a percentile of 42%, then 38% a year later, and 35% two years later.

The conclusion is inescapable: as the five-year cycle runs on, examinees get better at the current exam. One can argue that students are generally better prepared by our undergraduate programs, or that the exam comes to be a better measure of what is actually taught. Neither of these conclusions is reasonable. There is no evidence that all CS students, or all CS students likely to take the GRE/CS, are constantly improving. And one of the consistent complaints about the GRE/CS is that it is testing material that is either out of date or out of favor. The only argument for the better match with material taught is that the GRE/CS is gauged to fit leading-edge undergraduate programs, and so the majority catch up during the cycle. Perhaps. But there is another possibility that Occam's Razor promotes: students hear what was on the last exam, they study that, and—voila!—it's on the exam they take!

So in some sense the key is not old exams but old examinees. We would caution against quizzing your friends on what the questions were; after all, they agreed not to say. But they should be able to help with the scope of the exam.

What we can offer, and it is evanescent, is some impression of taking recent exams gathered by GRE/CS in spring 2000 and fall 2002, and by surveying students who took the exam from fall 2000 through fall 2001. (The survey form dealt with the scope of topics, *not* specific questions.) These results are incorporated throughout the following advice on reviewing content; when a large number of comments concern a particular subject area, you will find that fact noted there.

Chapter 3
Content Discussion
and Review

Content Discussion and Review

Programming languages

The good news is that there will be no questions on ANSI Pascal. It is no longer the popular choice for first language. High school Advanced Placement classes have switched to C++; now AP courses and many college introductory programming courses using C++ are moving to Java. There will probably never be questions on any language standard, for too many versions of too many languages are in widespread use. Thus, C, C++, Java, Scheme, ML, and who knows what others, share the spotlight of first programming language, with Pascal becoming an academic legacy (you can safely ignore the robot/turtle languages sometimes used to introduce programming). Perhaps you never even learned Pascal. Here are two good reasons to correct that: it is the pseudocode of choice (in fact, you may have learned it as pseudocode in an algorithms course) and it still is used on the GRE/CS. What? No contradiction—the questions now do not depend on knowing facts

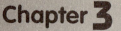

about the standard form but on being able to read code quickly. Consistent with the new tendency to explain problems, some questions even explain the Pascal syntax first. To summarize: Pascal still appears on the GRE/CS as pseudocode and in code fragment questions; knowing it speeds your reading of both types of problems. One could say the same of C/C++, but that is unlikely to be a weak area in your background.

What about other languages? Java is certainly popular, but familiarity with C++ should cover that. Some questions may still use a Fortran variant, and Lisp and Prolog will continue to exemplify functional and logic programming languages. Questions on the WWW were first noted in spring 2001, so one can expect to see HTML and probably Perl, as well as questions on core XML. It is possible that other scripting languages, such as Python and Tcl/Tk, will be mentioned soon. More network programming will appear, but probably not CORBA-COM and other higher layer codes. There will be more problems in parallel programming, but they will continue to be phrased in Pascal or C settings; MPI is not required. With regard to other APIs, it seems inevitable that OpenGL will make an appearance. But generally speaking, program fragments and language questions will be phrased in slight extensions of the usual languages—for example, admitting call-by-name to Pascal. Despite the growing professional need for TeX for journal submissions, it is unlikely that it will be covered on the GRE/CS because it is too specialized as a language, and undergraduates will not be required to use it anytime soon. Although MFC (on one end of the modernity spectrum) and Basic/VBasic and Cobol (on the other end) have large installed bases, they have no impact on the GRE/CS.

But there is another favorite programming language that has not been mentioned: assembly language. Although Intel and MIPS are the most popular, the few questions depending upon assembly will be digestible by practitioners of any version, and can probably be read in twice the time by those who have never programmed in assembly but can be reasonably imaginative about instruction mnemonics.

There are always problems on parameter passing, calls, and declaration scoping. You must know the distinctions among call by reference, value, name, and various combinations.

You must be familiar with the different ways variables are declared and where the declarations are valid. Global and local declarations, explicit and implicit typing, and overloading are all likely to come up. On the other hand, subtleties of binding in different forms of Lisp can be skipped.

Pointers are usually a stumbling block in learning to program, and they will always appear on the GRE/CS. You should be familiar with all aspects of pointer use and syntax in both Pascal and C, in case the problems are cast in some unfamiliar setting. The GRE/CS has a tendency to ask questions about one data structure that is implemented as another, such as using doubly-linked lists to implement deques. So it is not far-fetched that you would be asked about making pointers with arrays (just as Fortran had to do). Know allocation and deallocation, problems with null pointers, typing, and how to read pointers and their references.

There are always several code-fragment tracing problems. You are given a few lines of code and asked questions about the results of execution or the values returned if this is a procedure. Frequently, several questions relate to the same fragment. Sometimes you are asked to supply or correct a given line in the fragment to produce the stated result. You may be asked to identify the line that produces an error or that must be changed.

Reading code is a skill you must cultivate in any case, and you have been practicing it for years. Here is some helpful advice. Pay attention to the instructions, for there may be alterations or extensions to the syntax that are crucial. Do not be disturbed if the language appears to be unfamiliar—you are not expected to know every language. Sometimes you are being tested on the ability to read new code. The other examinees are just as likely to be as unfamiliar with it as you. Be confident and ignore the feeling that others are better prepared. It won't be true, and who cares anyway?

A few questions will be devoted to programming language principles and theoretical constructs. You may be asked to identify or compare different styles of parameter passing (call by name, value, reference, etc.), different semantics for programming languages (axiomatic, denotational, operational, etc.), different paradigms of languages (imperative, functional, declarative or logical, object-oriented). Except for the parameter-passing, which can involve some tricky code-tracing, the questions are typically of a factual character, and a conceptual review and common sense will probably suffice. See the section below on AI and Logic for more about logic programming languages.

Occasionally, there are questions on low-level languages, from assembly to embedded systems and even, in the past, to microcode. These questions can be answered by anyone with standard acquaintance with assembly language and will not tread into territories such as specialized interrupt or device programming, although more general knowledge of drivers and other systems-level software is fair game.

Expression evaluation

Frequent tasks on the exam include evaluations of expressions, traversals of syntax trees, and association of code fragments with calculations. Know the standard traversals and their connections with prefix, infix, and postfix notation. Know the standard operation precedence rules of mathematics, be aware that the precedence rules used differ among different programming languages, and observe that precedence also applies to logical or Boolean operations. Note that partial evaluation may affect the whole process, such as the first false value terminating the evaluation of the remaining parts of an AND expression. Then look for the introduction of novel rules or constraints in the problem, testing whether you can adapt your standard knowledge to new situations. The other sort of evaluation worth your training is general functional evaluation, as provided by the lambda calculus and implemented in Lisp.

Runtime data structures

Compilers and interpreters require runtime data structures to support the semantics of a programming language. Stacks, activation records, free-storage heaps, and hashing into symbol tables are examples; they may appear on the exam.

Bugs

You will find yourself confronting bugs during the GRE/CS, not because you will be writing code, but because several questions will depend on your recognizing and avoiding, or fixing, common ones.

Probably the most pervasive bug in computing is being off by one. My advice is do several small models, counting on your fingers. This should allow you to induce the pattern for the situation you face. A popular task is to ask how many numbers are represented by ... in the following:

1, 2, 3, 4, 5, ..., 10, ..., 100, ..., 1000.

Computer scientists know there is a problem here, and perhaps a fair share know the answers right away. I am not among them, but knowing the first gap is four numbers tells me immediately that the last answer is 899. Because of my inability to see these things, I always count (and always recommend it to students). The other part of the problem is recognizing when there is a hazard. Obvious cases are loop indexing, sequence counting, and execution tracing. But there may be others. If you see answer alternatives that differ by one, suspect the influence of this bug.

The other class of bugs worth studying deal with pointer references. We'll examine the C/C++ situation, and if you are more familiar with pointers in another language, learn how they work here. The first bug is the NULL pointer dereference, or attempting to find, directly or indirectly, what NULL points to, when in fact it does not point to anything at all. This is not so serious in programming, because the runtime system will catch the error. But it may appear in a problem. A similar fiasco is attempting to dereference a pointer that has been declared but not valued, but it's even worse to assign a reference value to a declared pointer without allocating memory (with new or malloc, or by assigning it NULL or another pointer). More trouble comes from trying to delete (the reference of) a pointer that has never been referenced, and from dereferencing a pointer after deleting an alias of it. For specifics on these and additional pointer bugs, try:

http://csis.pace.edu/~bergin/papers/PointerTraps.html

Verification, pre-/post-conditions, and loop invariants

There are typically questions about loop invariants, and less often about pre-/post-conditions in linear segments. These statements are written in a pseudocode or metalanguage in order to speak mathematically about status of variables, flags, loop indices, or other program parameters that may be changing in the loop or segment. They are inserted into the source code as comments, not executable statements. Program assertions of this type provide the framework for program verification. They are intended to be true statements at the time they are reached; that is, if we have

```
// precondition
<executable segment>
// postcondition
```

then the precondition is true before the indicated segment is executed, and the postcondition is true after.

In the case of a loop, which here seeks the index of the smallest element in a sequence:

```
indexMin = 0;
for(j = 1; j < sequence.length(); j++){
// loop invariant
if (sequence[j] < sequence[indexMin])
    indexMin = j;
}
```

the loop invariant is a statement that is true each time that marked position is reached during execution of the loop, and true when program control exits the loop. The following are all invariants for this loop:

- `j > 0`
- `j > indexMin`
- `0 <= indexMin`
- `for all k such that 0 <= k < j, sequence[k] <= sequence[indexMin]`

These invariants are listed in order of their relevance to characterizing the validity of the loop. The first is uninteresting, but the conjunction of the last three provides verification that the loop works. By contrast, the following are not loop invariants at the indicated position:

- `j > 1`
- `0 < indexMin`
- `for all k such that 0 <= k < j, sequence[k] > sequence[indexMin]`
- `j < sequence.length()`

The first two *start out* false, but may become true; the third is *always* false; and the fourth is true until *after* the exit.

Algorithms

Most algorithm performance questions are phrased in terms of Θ, because that allows mutually exclusive alternatives to be easily stated. In short, for functions f, g on N, the natural numbers, $f = \Theta(g)$ means that there are positive real constants c_1, c_2, and a natural number M, such that for all $n \geq M$,

$$0 \leq c_1 g(n) \leq f(n) \leq c_2 g(n).$$

This is equivalent to saying $g = \Theta(f)$. Indeed, we can view Θ as an equivalence relation, usually on N^N. Whenever c_2 exists above, we write $f = O(g)$, and whenever c_1 exists above, we write $f = \Omega(g)$, which is the same as $g = O(f)$. Consequently, other characterizations of $f = \Theta(g)$ are:

$$f = O(g) \ \& \ g = O(f)$$

or

$$f = O(g) \ \& \ f = \Omega(g).$$

It is unlikely that there will be any questions about $f = o(g)$ or $f = \omega(g)$, but in order to be complete, take $f = o(g)$ to mean that for *every* positive real number c, there exists some $M > 0$, such that for all $n \geq M$,

$$0 \leq f(n) \leq cg(n).$$

Then $f = \omega(g)$ means $g = o(f)$. There has been no use on the GRE/CS lately of O, Ω, o, or ω, but characterizations are included because it is likely you have seen some of them, and because it is too easy to be confused by them. So don't worry, be happy, and figure you will only see Θ.

The big trend is to state all algorithm problems precisely in terms of Θ, rather than in more verbose English. The algorithm questions fall into three categories: construction, identification, and analysis. Algorithm construction is exemplified by pseudocode-tracing to determine properties of the algorithm implemented or to correct an incorrectly implemented algorithm. Identification involves naming the algorithm implemented, ranking algorithms (by time or space requirements, for example) when you are given a list of names, and matching named algorithms and properties. Analysis focuses on determining speed or other properties, given the specification of an algorithm by pseudocode or description. Θ will appear in the last two, and pseudocode may be involved in all three types. Specific concepts required are the various searches and sorts (including those on data structures other than indexed sequences such as tries, B-trees, heaps), hash functions and collision policies, graph and tree processing (with attention to traveling salesperson problems, minimal spanning tree, graph and tree traversals). Because the fall 2002 exam I took has a large number of questions depending on trees and graphs, I would recommend some extra aquaintance with definitions and uses here.

A clear distinction must be made among best, worst, and average cases. Comparisons of the fast sorts (heapsort, quicksort, mergesort) are the basis of many questions, and you should memorize time behaviors in all cases. But there may be novel algorithms that you are expected to clock or to distinguish by best and/or worst cases.

Standard algorithms may be extended to unexpected data structures; for example, you may face a question about an algorithm that appears to be binary search, but it is applied to an unordered, unkeyed structure, such as an unsorted linked list, where it does not have $\Theta(\log n)$ speed at all. The lesson is that identification of the algorithm and recall of its properties do not finish the problem.

Another more devious type of problem is unobvious code that turns out to compute a common algorithm, or code that appears to be a standard algorithmic routine, but instead computes something different.

Recurrence relations

Recurrence relations frequently lead to explicit solutions for timing algorithms. They may not be required in the algorithm problems, but they often appear themselves as topics of questions. You need to be familiar with a few simple examples of solving recurrence relations, which will provide adequate review of the basic methods and tie them to concrete applications. Sometimes recurrence relations can be guessed, and correcting a guess is one heuristic method for solving them. Looking for empirical patterns on small values does sometimes help. But you will not be able to identify the underlying mechanism on sight from the recurrence information, and there will be attractive and logical distractors. So skill in math will avoid a bad guess.

Mathematics

The next section highlights math content. For those most intent on succeeding on the exam, this is to be supplemented by mathematical problem-solving skills review and enhancement. But why so much math here? If you are like my own students, you retain CS concepts, recall them, and use them with facility, but basic discrete math—taught in several courses—is not so readily evidenced in class discussions and, most importantly, on tests. Given this, and the argument earlier for math skills, I now would like to expand the math discussion.

Calculation and estimation

The primary mathematical requirement is the ability to calculate. This includes accurate and fast arithmetical operations on integers and rationals expressed in decimal and binary/octal/ hexadecimal form. You should be familiar with converting among these bases, and have some practice with others. Fractions, floating point numbers, and radicals may appear in calculations.

Care must be taken in estimating to make sure that the estimate excludes distractors. Saving a few digits' worth of arithmetic is not worth it if you fall prey to a wrong answer. This is particularly true in percent calculations; you should be completely comfortable in all uses of percent, for it appears on every exam with classically trapping distractors. Markup and discount, couched as delay or speedup for example, are particularly popular. Laws governing exponents and logarithms merit review, so that changing from one log base to another holds no ambiguity for you.

You will be reminded of set designations $\{x : 3x < 25\}$ and operations like $R \cup S$, $R \cap S$, $R - S$, and $R \times S$ at the front of the exam. This should be unnecessary, for you must be fluent in the set theoretic notation and description of computing concepts, including the characterization of relations, functions, size of infinite sets, and structures such as graphs, trees, and Cartesian products. Topics that have been selected to be reviewed are: relations and functions and their iteration, some operations on sets, and the counting of sets. These specific topics are chosen to set the level of sophistication recommended for your preparation for the exam rather than for their particular likeliness to appear.

Relations, functions, and algebras

A relation R from A to B is a subset of $A{\times}B$, that is, $R \in P(A{\times}B)$.

$R^{-1} = \{(x,y) : (y,x) \in R\}$ is the converse, or inverse.

The domain of R is $\text{Dom}(R) = \{x : \exists y \ (x,y) \in R\}$, the range of R, $\text{Rng}(R)$, is the domain of R^{-1}. The field of R is $\text{Dom}(R) \cup \text{Rng}(R)$. R is a unary function if $(a,b), (a,c) \in R \Rightarrow b = c$. To indicate that R is a function, we write $R : \text{Dom}(R){\to}C$, where C is any set including $\text{Rng}(R)$. In general, n-ary functions are $(n+1)$-ary relations R that satisfy

$$(a_1,a_2,...,a_n,b), (a_1,a_2,...,a_n,c) \in R \Rightarrow b = c.$$

If $f{:}A{\to}B$ is a unary function, then f is 1–1 if the converse relation f^{-1} is a function; f is onto if $f(A) = \text{Rng}(f) = B$.

Assume A, B are finite sets. Every 1–1 $f{:}A{\to}A$ is onto. Similarly, if $|A| > |B|$, then $f{:}A{\to}B$ cannot be 1–1. These observations are commonly called the Pigeonhole Principle. For arbitrary sets X, Y, there exists a 1–1 onto $g{:}X{\to}Y$ (a 1–1 correspondence) *iff* $|X| = |Y|$.

Functions, equivalences, and orders are the most important types of relations for computer science. Master these operations on relations:

$R{\circ}S = \{(x,y) : \exists z \ ((x,z) \in R \ \& \ (z,y) \in S)\}$, the composition, or relative product;

$R^R = R \cup \{(x,x) : \exists y \ ((x,y) \in R \text{ or } (y,x) \in R\}$, the reflexive closure;

$R^S = R \cup R^{-1}$, the symmetric closure;

$R^T = \cup\{R^n : n \geq 1\}$, the transitive closure,

where $R^{k+1} = R \circ R^k$;

$R^E = R^{RST}$, the equivalence relation generated by R.

Equivalences range from equality to the trivial equivalence, $A \times A$. Each partitions the domain into disjoint, exhaustive equivalence classes. Every function $f:A \rightarrow B$ establishes an equivalence on A:

$a \sim b \Leftrightarrow f(a) = f(b)$.

Conversely, given any equivalence R, we define the quotient function that maps $\text{Dom}(R)$ onto the set of R-equivalence classes:

$q(a) = [a]_R = \{x : xRa\}$. Then, $\sim_q = R$.

An order (or, partial order) is a relation $\leq$ that is reflexive, transitive, and antisymmetric: $a \leq b$ & $b \leq a \Rightarrow a = b$. Among orders, the total, well, and lattice orders have particular significance for computing.

A total order is also called a linear order, where any two elements are comparable: $a \leq b \vee b \leq a$. A special case of total order is the well order, in which every descending chain $a_0 \geq a_1 \geq a_2 \geq \ldots$ is finite. The natural numbers and the ordinal numbers are the most important examples.

A lattice is an order where greatest lower bound (glb or meet, ·) and least upper bound (lub or join, +) define two binary associative and commutative operations that satisfy:

$$a+a = a \cdot a = a \text{ (idempotency)}$$
$$(a + b) \cdot b = a \cdot b + b = b \text{ (absorption)}$$

Conversely, the laws mentioned characterize algebras in which order can be defined by

$$a \leq b \text{ iff } a \cdot b = a \text{ (or, equivalently, } a+b = b),$$

and then meet and join are recaptured as the glb and lub. The most familiar examples of lattices are Boolean algebras, ignoring the complement operation, and total orders (chains).

There is likely to be little coverage of any other types of algebras. Although groups are vital in studying codes and semigroups are essential for understanding string processing, many students do not cover abstract algebra in discrete math. The only area of "modern" algebra likely to be familiar to all students and quite likely to appear on the exam is linear algebra.

The vector spaces R^n are the usual subjects, usually R^2 and R^3. Problems frequently involve matrices. LU decomposition, determinant equations, and matrices with two or so variable elements are popular. Be ready for manipulations such as addition, multiplication, and forming the inverse (you probably will not be expected to do this via (det A)$^{-1}$ * adj A, but it works). Fundamental notions of bases of various types, linear transformations (and their matrices), kernels, and dimension calculations are plausible. Do not dwell on more advanced information about abstract vector spaces, linear transformations, and duality.

Turning to iteration of functions, these problems appear to be similar to recurrence relations, but are quite distinct in method and result. For example, assume $f(0) = 0$, $f(1) = 2$, and for $n > 1$, $f(n) = f(f(n-2))+1$. Then we show $f(5) = f(4)-1$. First, compute $f(2)$: $f(2) = f(f(0))+1 = f(0)+1 = 0+1 = 1$. Then

$$f(4) = f(f(2))+1 = f(1)+1 = 2+1 = 3,$$
$$f(5) = f(f(3))+1 = f(f(f(1))+1)+1 = f(1+1)+1$$
$$= f(2)+1 = 1+1 = 2.$$

Set theory

In addition to the usual set-theoretic operations of union, intersection, complement or difference, and Cartesian product, you should be aware of some facts and uses of the symmetric difference $A\Delta B$ and power A^B of two sets A and B. The former is defined as the difference of the union and the intersection: $A\Delta B = (A\cup B) - (A\cap B)$; it is commutative and associative: $A\Delta B = B\Delta A$, $(A\Delta B)\Delta C = A\Delta(B\Delta C)$. The critical property is a self-inversion: $A\Delta B\Delta B = A$, which can be viewed as a consequence of $B\Delta B = \varnothing$. If union is an expression of logical OR, and intersection is related to AND, then Δ captures XOR: $A\Delta B = \{x : x\in A \text{ XOR } x\in B\}$. A useful property is $\cap$-distributivity: $(A\Delta B)\cap C = (A\cap C)\Delta(B\cap C)$; the other intersection form and those with union do not hold.

The power A^B is the set of functions with domain B and the range included in A: $A^B = \{f \mid f:B\to A\}$. If we take $2 = \{0,1\}$, then 2^B is the set of characteristic functions f for $C \subseteq B$: $f(x) = 1$ if $x \in C$, and 0 if $x \in B-C$. Thus, 2^B can be identified via a natural 1–1 correspondence with $P(B)$. We obtain equations $|2^B| = |P(B)| = 2^{|B|}$ that hold for finite and infinite sets alike.

Counting strings and subsets

Suppose A is a finite alphabet, and S is a set of strings (finite sequences of letters) using the letters of A; S is usually called a language over A. Observe that if the strings in S have bounded length n, then $|S|$, the cardinality or size of S, is finite and can be no larger than $|A|^n$. If S has no such bound, then S is countably infinite, having cardinality of N, the natural numbers. If A is infinite, and S has a bound on length of $n \geq 1$, then still $|S| \leq |A|^n$, but now this is just $|A|$. If S has no such bound, then $|S|$ still has a maximum size of $|A|$. If A has cardinality of R, the real numbers (unlikely in computer science), then so can S. Note the special case when A is empty: $|S| = 0$ or 1, depending on whether S is empty or includes only the empty string. The following table summarizes the size of the set $T(A)$ of all strings over the alphabet A, for various sizes of A, and then gives the size of the set $T_n(A)$ of all strings over A of string length $n \in N$:

$|A|$	$|T(A)|$	$|T_n(A)|$
0	1	1, if $n = 0$
		0, otherwise
$m \in N, m \geq 1$	$|N|$	m^n
$|N|$	$|N|$	1, if $n = 0$
		$|N|$, otherwise
$|R|$	$|R|$	$|R|$

Let's turn to counting subsets. This becomes important when formal languages are discussed, because they are sets of strings, and one may wish to know how many languages of a particular kind there are. If a set has m elements, then the number of subsets is 2^m. This holds whether m is a natural number (including 0) or an infinite number (we take $|R| = 2^{|N|}$). The following table gives the size of the set $P(A)$ of all languages for a given size of alphabet A, of the set $P_n(A)$ for string length n, and of the set $P_{fin}(A)$ of finite subsets of $T(A)$.

$|A|$	$|P(A)|$	$|P_n(A)|$	$|P_{fin}(A)|$
0	2	2, if $n = 0$ 1, otherwise	2
$m \in N,\ m \geq 1$	$|R|$	2^{m^n}	$|N|$
$|N|$	$|R|$	2, if $n = 0$ $|R|$, otherwise	$|N|$
$|R|$	$2^{|R|}$	2, if $n = 0$ $2^{|R|}$, otherwise	$|R|$

Example: How many languages of even palindromes on two letters (strings read the same forwards and backwards and have even length)? So $A = \{a,b\}$, and $T(A)$ is countably infinite. The set $EP(A)$ of all even palindromes is in 1–1 correspondence with $T(A)$ by associating, e.g., babaabab with baba. So the number of subsets of $EP(A)$ is the same as the number of subsets of $T(A)$, and is similarly uncountable.

The counting review will be continued during the discussion of automata and formal languages.

Combinatorics

Beyond counting for cardinality lies combinatorics, the counting of different combinations of attributes. The basic notions are the count

$$P(n,k) = n!/(n-k)!$$

of the number of ways to pick an ordered list of k items from a set of n items (no repeats!), and the count

$$C(n,k) = n!/(k!(n-k)!)$$

of the number of ways to choose an unordered set of k items from a set of n items. A simple way to keep track is to see the set selected filling a sequence of boxes: [ ][ ][ ][ ][ ][ ], then writing in the number of things that could go in each place in turn; so for $P(7,4)$, this tableau is [7][6][5][4]. $P(7,4)$ is just the product of these counts. If the unordered selection count $C(7,4)$ is needed, then divide $P(7,4)$ by the count of the ways to reorder the four boxes, namely $P(4,4) = 4!$. But keep in mind that in these arrangements, no repetition is allowed. For repetition: there are n^k ways to fill k boxes from a set of n items, copies allowed. So, taking $\{0,1\}$ as the item supply, there are $[2][2][2] = 2^3 = 8$ binary strings of length 3.

Discrete probability

After you can count, you can calculate probabilities. You count the multiplicities of outcomes, such as the different ways to get sums of the faces of two dice, and take the probability to be the relative frequency, for example:

$$P(\text{sum} = 7) = 6/36.$$

This then gives a probability distribution for a discrete random variable, in this example the function that takes two dice to the sum of their faces.

By the nature of computation, discrete probability plays a major role in computerized models and simulations. Discrete and continuous probability distributions P are distinguished by the former assigning nonnegative real-number probabilities to the real-numerical (often integer) values of a random variable V over a finite sample space S under the condition that the sum of these probabilities is 1.0. Thus,

$$\sum_{t \in V(S)} P(V=t) = 1.0.$$

When V is a continuous random variable over an infinite sample space, then the probability of any single-value event is zero:

$$P(V=t) = 0.0 \text{ for all } t \in V(S).$$

The main application is using the computationally tractable versions (models) of the former to approximate (simulate) the latter. The process is present in divergent settings, from finite-element analysis in mechanics to implicit surface subdivision in geometry. Of course, there are other uses of discrete probability and many other types of computer modeling, but this is the central example.

Graphs

Graphs expressed as node sets plus edge sets are popular data structures with several different internal representations. They are used for conveying and studying a broad class of algorithmic problems. They have had a very strong presence on several recent exams. It is wise to be familiar with common notions and techniques, and it is possible that you will be required to recall specific graph algorithms.

You will need to know the definition of directed acyclic graph (DAG), bipartite graph, complete graph, and tree/forest. Among the last, there is often reference to binary search trees. Tree traversal questions appear on every exam. You are also likely to meet a small but nonzero number of problems based on some standard search task in a graph, e.g., shortest path, Hamiltonian or Eulerian circuit, minimal spanning tree, or graph coloring. It will not hurt to read algorithms and practice them on some small graphs. That way, even if the task is new, you will be prepared.

Trees as data structures deserve a few lines (with more at Algorithms) and lengthier study. Binary trees are the basic configuration. To be efficient for access and other operations, a tree should be balanced, with all the paths from root to leaves of nearly equal lengths. Balancing characteristics, strategies, operations, and implementations vary, as exemplified by red-black, height-balanced, and AVL trees. Balanced trees are advantageous as indexes, search trees, and other applications. The B-tree generalizes the balanced binary tree by allowing nodes to have many children, usually globally bounded above and below. The high branching degree facilitates efficient retrieval of keyed data from slow secondary storage. For example, a B-tree with a height of 3 and a branching factor of 1001 can store more than one trillion keys but requires, at most, three disk accesses to search for any node.

Logic

Familiarity with logical notation for propositional and predicate calculus is helpful, but use of truth tables, especially those associated with the connectives AND, OR, NAND, NOR, IF...THEN, XOR, and IFF is required. Alternate forms of notation are used for these; for example, *A* AND *B* may be written *A* & *B*, $A \wedge B$, $A \cdot B$, or *AB*. Although the notational conventions are given at the beginning of the test, you should be familiar with ones from past tests and alternatives before entering the exam room. This is not the time to pore over the notational conventions hoping to figure out the distinction between XOR and AND. As mentioned earlier, you need to be familiar with Boolean calculation as well as binary.

Also fruitful for questions is the interplay between Boolean values and binary arithmetic. Because carry bits are so important in architecture, there may be Boolean or binary arithmetic problems that stress them. An example of the use of XOR is given by one-bit add-carry. Let *A*, *B* be 1-bit Boolean variables. Then the sum bit of *A*+*B* is *A* XOR *B*, and the carry bit is *A* AND *B*.

With regard to principles of logic, the most typical appearances involve distributivity:

A AND (*B* OR *C*) IFF (*A* AND *B*) OR (*A* AND *C*),
A OR (*B* AND *C*) IFF (*A* OR *B*) AND (*A* OR *C*);

or, written as Boolean algebraic expressions:

$a(b+c) = ab+ac$,
$a + bc = (a+b)(a+c)$.

The contrast emphasizes the above point of being familiar with the alternative notations. The other property frequently seen is DeMorgan's laws:

$\neg(A \wedge B) \Leftrightarrow \neg A \vee \neg B$,
$\neg(A \vee B) \Leftrightarrow \neg A \wedge \neg B$,

with the latter derived from the former via double negation:

$\neg\neg A \Leftrightarrow A$,

in the usual notation for propositional logic.

Putting Boolean expressions (in the language of lattices, propositional calculus, etc.) into a minimized form is a perennial task on the exam. This may be presented as a normal form problem and now more rarely as a Karnaugh map. Be familiar with some technique, for you can usually use the one you prefer with minimal translation.

See also the section below on AI and Logic for more about logic programming.

We close this section with a puzzle that looks like a legitimate but strange GRE/CS problem. It will test your logic.

The following question, in *italic,* appeared on a multiple-choice examination in which each question was guaranteed to have a unique correct answer. Identify the correct answer and explain why the other answers cannot be correct.

[17] *Assume I and II are statements that have well-defined truth values, i.e., each statement is either true or false and not both. Then this question on the test can be answered without further information, since there must be a unique correct answer.*

(A) *I and II are both false.*
(B) *I is false and II is true.*
(C) *I is true and II is false.*
(D) *I and II are both true.*
(E) *If I is false, then II is false.*

Let's maintain the puzzle, but here is a clue, if needed. The trick is to make sure (E) is not true.

Numerical computation

Number representations

You must be familiar with computer representation of integers, real numbers, and alphanumeric strings. Binary representation of integers with ones-complement and twos-complement conventions should be supplemented with octal and hexadecimal bases. Keep a clear distinction between this and binary block codes of other types of symbols; examples are the historic BCD and current ASCII and Unicode. Related to this is the question of byte order in multibyte words, typically big-endian or little-endian. Other implemented bases include ternary (with coefficients, or trits, 0,1,2), balanced ternary (with coefficients –1,0,1), and biquinary (with dual coefficients of 0,1 picking the half-decade and 0,1,2,3,4 within it)—even decimal, but that presents fewer problems, not more. These historical backwaters are old ideas that provide broad possibilities for unfamiliar questions. Your robustness will improve if you consider them: it will not harm you to know some history, and will serve to break the impression that CS is monolithically modernistic. In other words, it is dead wrong to assume that the only gaps in your knowledge will stem from what you do not yet know about today's methodology and technology.

Floating-point representation will undoubtedly appear on the exam, as it has on every one we have seen or studied. Given a representation, know the range of numbers represented approximately and exactly. The former depends on the exponent, and the latter on both the mantissa and the exponent. For example, 1/3 cannot be exactly represented in binary or decimal floating point, but is no problem in ternary. Pay attention to how the sign is encoded—usually, there will be distractors fishing for wrong sign interpretation.

Once you have the numbers represented, be ready to convert from base to base, including binary to hex or octal, as well as to and from decimal. Be ready to do simple arithmetic in binary: addition, subtraction, multiplication. Even if you are familiar with floating point in binary, octal, or hex, you may have misgivings on seeing 0.011; it is important to think of base-10 and base-2 positional notation as similar. Indeed

$$0.011_{10} = 0*10^{-1}+1*10^{-2}+1*10^{-3}, \text{ and}$$

$$0.011_2 = 0*2^{-1} + 1*2^{-2} + 1*2^{-3} = 0.375_{10}$$

and these behave as sums of powers in exactly the same way. As a last stimulating example, you can have a positional notation without powers of a fixed base, or radix; here is the factorial mixed-radix system:

$$3221_! = 0*0! + 1*1! + 2*2! + 2*3! + 3*4! = 89_{10};$$

in general, for $n \geq 0$, the nth term is $a_n*n!$ with $0 \leq a_n \leq n$, and a_0 always 0. Another use of a mixed radix system is our keeping time as

ww:d:hh:mm:ss.

Finiteness of representation

Ignored in the previous paragraph are the penalties incurred by having finite (and usually fixed) register and word length. You must be familiar with round-off, overflow, and underflow, and how these can interact with choices of representation, especially fixed vs. floating and ones- vs. twos-complement. Be aware of how round-off policies (off, up, down, truncation) differ and how they

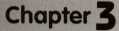
apply to negative numbers. This is a good place to mention facility with the floor and ceiling operators, which offer good and frequent problems.

Linear algebra and numerical methods

Each of these is usually an entire course. That's how I can get away with throwing them into a single paragraph. From the former, bring facility with vectors and matrices and more than a little practice with Gaussian elimination and a few computer-related techniques like LU factorization and matrix inverse computation.

Numerical analysis is far less likely to be required or taken. But a quick study of polynomial evaluation and Newton's method will give some background on two of the most common applications: function evaluation and root finding. Scientific computation may provide more questions in the future, but this is not an economical area for fruitful review.

Automata and the theory of computation

A number of questions on every exam involve finite automata, formal languages, Turing machines, and computation theory. Many students tend to overrate their number; according to the guidelines given by ETS, automata and language theory are one of a group of three topics to which 25% of the questions are devoted, so 8–10%, or an absolute number of about 5–7 questions, seems right. A typical problem is, given a machine or grammar, trace its behavior. Regular expressions combined with other characterizations of regular languages are also popular. In addition, there have been frequent test questions about the hierarchies of machines and languages or problems. This table summarizes the basics:

Machine	Grammar	Det vs. Nondet	Chomsky type
FA	Regular	Same	3
NondetPDA	Context free	Weaker	2
NondetLBA	Context sensitive	Weaker	1
Turing decide		Same	0 Recursive
Turing accept	Unlimited	Same	0 Rec. enumerable

Another frequent category of questions focuses on closure properties. First note that all classes of languages considered are closed under union, concatenation, and Kleene * closure (iterated concatenation).

Language	Intersection	Complement
Regular (RL)	Yes	Yes
Context-free (CFL)	No	No
Context-sensitive (CSL)	Yes	Yes
Recursive (Rec.)	Yes	Yes
Recursively enumerable (R.e.)	Yes	No

Note that the intersection of a CFL and RL is CFL.

Because there are only countably infinite many distinct machines of each category, the languages they characterize are also no more than countably infinite in number. It is easily shown that there are at least that many as well. Over a nonempty alphabet, there are uncountably many languages, so uncountably many languages will escape each of the characterizations.

Your review should stress grammars, machines, and some basic recursive function theory. For the last, you should know the following:

A. Halting problems for Turing machines are largely recursively unsolvable (but, for example, the Turing acceptor for a recursive set has a solvable halting problem).

B. Recursively enumerable sets have alternative characterizations as languages accepted or semidecided by Turing machines, domains of partial recursive functions, ranges of partial recursive functions, ranges of total recursive functions (for nonempty r.e. sets), and ranges of 1–1 recursive functions (for infinite r.e. sets).

C. If A is the range of a strictly monotonic recursive function f, that is

$$x < y \Rightarrow f(x) < f(y),$$

then A is recursive. If A and its complement are both r.e., then A is recursive.

You should know the distinction between P and NP and the import of NP-complete problems. It is not worth reviewing much detail though; in other words, 3SAT is an example of an NP-complete problem, but it is unlikely that there will be a question about 3SAT or any other specific problem. You need not worry much about other complexity classes (such as PSpace, ExpTime).

Operating systems

Because OS is likely to be the last of a series of CS courses—and the most advanced nonmathematical course that every CS graduate is likely to have—there is considerable focus on operating systems on the GRE/CS. Students taking the exam report this to be one of the more intensely covered areas. Perhaps the best news is that most questions yield to CS commonsense analysis. You will need the concepts and techniques from a course, but you will have undoubtedly had one. We give a quick review here of the relevant areas.

Resource allocation and scheduling

The key to these problems is reading carefully and drawing diagrams. Alternatives are usually quickly reduced because some are simply inconsistent with the given data or constraints. Despite the suggestion that some principle will be needed to select the correct alternative, it usually happens that only one remains as consistent with the given information.

Memory management and virtual memory

There are always several questions on virtual memory (VM) and paging. Pages are the virtual concept, as realized in peripheral memory. Page frames are the real concept, blocks of main memory. VM maps pages to page frames. Often there is an example of finding an address on a loaded page, given the VM parameters for it. The practice problems cover this. The key is to have the concepts straight: only a loaded page has a memory address, so don't be confused by how many pages are not in local memory.

Another type of problem deals with page replacement and the order of mapping pages to memory, based on some scheduling scheme, e.g., replace the eldest (FIFO), replace the least recently used (LRU), etc. For these, also note the advice above for scheduling and resource allocation. Be aware that true LRU is not feasible, for it would require constant counting in the OS, so hardware support provides a rolling record of touched pages. Distinguish between used-but-clean and dirty pages, the latter being rewritten. Several recent questions have related to details such as the TLB (translation lookaside buffer, which allows fast reference to related addresses without OS calls), page tables, and PTE (page table entries).

Finally, be prepared for questions on the overall mechanism of virtual memory, why it is useful, and what the costs are.

Concurrent computation

If concurrent programming appears, it will be in a code fragment where synchronization primitives occur. Working through some examples in any text, usually OS, will provide you with the required background and practice.

When it comes to OS support for concurrency, then typical topics are control structures, deadlock, and synchronization. Deadlock is a common topic for questions, even if real OSs ignore it. You should be familiar with the methods for inviting deadlock and for avoiding it. Semaphores and blocking, useful for synchronization of simultaneous resource requests and concurrent activities (processes, tasks, threads), lead to it. Generally, avoidance is sought through some attack on one or more of the prerequisites. Mutual exclusion cannot be eliminated, but circularity can. Each technique mentioned has advantages and costs; you should be familiar with these.

Other areas

You should be familiar with distinctions among processes, tasks, and threads. File structures and different types of access to files, input-output buffers, and design tradeoff between size and speed will appear. Learn or review the distinction between sequential and random access file structures and why different storage media favor each. A common question type rests on knowing how file access time depends on the speed of different subtasks; for example, a disk's rotational velocity, different timings for positioning the head and stepping tracks, cylinder vs. sector, and so forth.

Computer architecture

Representation of data and instructions

Concerning representation of numerical data in binary formats, see the discussion under math, but if you need a printed reference, check your architecture text. For general data, the current models are ASCII and Unicode, neither of which will be tested. But you may see a question on a coding scheme concocted for the exam, so familiarity with one will make the novel case more comfortable. For instructions, there may be a cluster of problems concerning a specific instruction set and instruction word format specified in sufficient detail in the exam itself. The best way to approach such a problem is to be familiar with some instruction architecture, and even better, more than one. Also, see the discussion that follows on RISC.

Caching

Caching appears on the exam regularly. Often the task is to distinguish among the three main techniques: direct mapping, fully associative, and the blended set-associative. A further distinction of type is between write-through, which updates cache and memory at the same time, and the less effective but easier to implement write-back, which updates memory only when the cache line is ejected. Level I is distinguished from Level II by being part of the CPU (as opposed to being on the motherboard, or even on the CPU assembly more frequently today), and by providing a division between instruction caching (usually not modified) and data caching. The biggest expense factor for CPUs is the cache.

Memory hierarchy

The memory hierarchy has at least six levels in today's computing systems:

Registers,
Level I cache,
Level II cache (and maybe more levels),
Main memory (e.g., RAM),
Secondary memory and virtual memory (e.g., hard disk),
Archival

These are ordered in decreasing speed of access, speed of reading and writing, expense, and proximity to the CPU. The first three are now often part of the CPU assembly. Besides questions that may refer specifically to properties of registers or cache, there is usually a question comparing two or more of these memory types. There may be additional instances of memory store as well. The CPU usually has some built-in code, for example, to implement complex instructions in the CISC case; an historical example is the microcode that implemented the entire machine instruction set in fast, simple manipulations of parts of bytes. More recent and now universal are ROM stores of code that implement the low levels of the input/output (such as BIOS) and CMOS Tables that store the machine configurations. Peripherals and their hardware controller cards will have their own memories, some for data, some for code.

Digital design

Boolean algebra and similar issues are covered in the earlier math sections, but you might want to be familiar with simple constructs and circuits such as adders, in particular, ripple-carry and carry-lookahead ones. Aspects and components of ALUs and other subunit designs are important, including multiplexers, decoders, latches, and flip-flops. Such questions have appeared on recent exams, but this area is not likely to produce more than two or three.

Performance enhancement

Efforts continue to get average completion of one instruction per cycle. Of course, the context is a serial CPU, rather than parallel or vector architectures. The typical method is pipelining with either branch prediction or delayed branching. Two new approaches are multiple-issue (or superscalar) architectures, which identify upcoming noninteracting instructions that can be executed independently and in parallel. New technology employs VLIW (very long instruction words) to allow the compiler to pack instructions in a single word for superscalar execution. This is a reversal of the tendency to dedicate all performance enhancement in the hardware to runtime, now allowing the compiler to schedule the improvement. Another modern strategy is predicated instructions, which avoid the pipeline flush of the failed branch prediction by maintaining the pipeline but using a flag bit to turn the effect of the currently executing instruction into a NOP if it is not on the computed branch.

Reduced Instruction Set Computers

There have been GRE/CS questions recently on RISC, as distinguished from CISC (Complex Instruction Set Computers). This is predictable given the popularity of the Patterson and Hennessy computer organization and architecture books, which introduced the MIPS RISC architecture, but students who have not studied these books or RISC at all have become alarmed. You should not be confused if you have not studied RISC. The questions yield to common sense, once you know a minimum about reduced instruction set methodology. Here is the core: short uniform instruction format (single-word length instruction using the same bits for each op-code for faster instruction decoding), uniform register addressing in every context (for simpler compiling), and simplified address modes, replacing the complex modes of CISC instructions (Intel, for example) with chains of simpler operations. Typical implementations allow a single clock, which together with the fixed length instruction word-support pipelining; using registers more than main memory and separating LOAD and STORE operations promote faster access and reuse of data. Overall, there is a savings on hardware at the cost of software; executable code will typically be longer than CISC, but the program may well run faster because of the optimizations mentioned.

Input/output

In addition to the file formats and buffers mentioned earlier, it may help to know something about interrupts, direct memory addressing (DMA), and polling.

Performance analysis

Amdahl's law has been sighted on recent exams. You should also be aware of systems performance analysis, in terms of system throughput under light, heavy, and saturating loads.

Chapter 4
More Specialized Knowledge

More
Specialized
Knowledge

Data communication

Networks

Although TCP/IP on Ethernet dominates on installed LANs, with bridges, switches, routers, and servers supplying the infrastructure for local and Internet connections, it is worth reviewing other approaches such as token-ring, star, and hardwired completely connected peer-to-peer networks.

Protocols

The default, de facto standard of TCP/IP and elaborations of these midlayer protocols have both overshadowed and informed the standard: ISO OSI (for Open Systems Interconnection model), the famed seven-layer architecture. Although

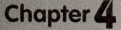
the seven layers (and even more) remain, the OSI protocols themselves have been overwhelmed by TCP/IP. Regardless, such distinctions have nothing to do with the GRE/CS; general knowledge of protocol stacks should prove sufficient. Just remember TCP is the prominent example of a reliable protocol, and UDP is the standard example of an unreliable one. Be familiar with stop-and-wait vs. pipelined protocols.

Bandwidth

Typical questions include how long it takes to transfer a file of certain size characteristics across a channel of a given bandwidth. There may be added error detection/correction bits and protocol overhead. Some percent of packets may be lost, with retransmission timing required. As long as you understand the concepts, the problem reduces to easy arithmetic. Beware of putting too much into such problems; there is often an extraneous quantity that should be ignored, but there will be a distractor for using it.

You should be aware of the differences in speed (not particular speeds) among twisted-pair POTS lines, conditioned phone lines, leased lines such as T1 and E1, coaxial cable, optical fiber, and wireless and radio data communication channels. Latency and transfer times are also influenced by satellite hops, so expect that to be a possible source of questions. At a higher level, detail on newer technologies like fast Ethernet, ATM, frame relay, and optical multiplexing will not be required, but such notions may appear in content questions that compare different networking solutions.

Encryption, compression, and error correction

It is unlikely that encryption will have any particular impact on the exam, but other kinds of coding could be introduced into a question on data transfer. Besides error detection/correction, which will probably be confined to CRC or checksum, you should know something about compression, such as a simple variable-length frequency coding with prefix-unique strings (Huffman codes), or run-length encoding. Gray codes plus basic notions of error-detecting and -correcting may be useful. Cryptology gets next to no attention on the GRE/CS.

AI and Logic

Heuristic search

Heurisitic search is usually considered to be an alternative to exhaustive search—especially when optimal search is known to be infeasible: for instance, exponential in the length of the key. Even for exhaustive optimal search, AI typically employs guided techniques such as branch and bound (especially α-β pruning in game trees) and dynamic programming. For suboptimal searches, besides a number of approximate but provably adequate algorithms, the usual process involves some variation on hill-climbing to maximize a measure of relevance, or minimize a metric distance from a goal.

Logic programming

Unification (such as finding the most general unifier) and clausal resolution (such as unit resolution of Horn clauses) have appeared in questions. You may have encountered these in AI, Logic, or Principles of Programming Languages courses, especially during discussions of logic programming languages such as Prolog.

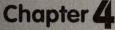

Circuit logic

Combinatorial circuits

Without timing signals, these can be converted directly into Boolean or logical expressions, which may offer some a more managable view of the problem. Remember that gate symbols appear in the convention list in the instruction part of the exam booklet, so you do not have to memorize the symbols, only the behavior.

Clocked circuits

When timing signals are present, a wholly different set of tasks are presented. Without hesitation, I reveal a secret heuristic: despite several courses in EE, I know nothing about such digital circuits, and I have never found it helpful to read the solutions to the problems. So I cannot be helpful, but I do offer it as an example of an area where skipping the problem is the clear choice. Perhaps your blind spots are elsewhere, and you can analyze clocked circuits intuitively and quickly. Do not hesitate to admit you have a blind spot somewhere—either fix the ignorance or skip the problems with joy. I expect you, however, to limit this advice to only one or two blind spots.

Specialized computing

Parallel computation

It is unlikely that more than one question will relate to parallel computing. Be aware of distinctions between instruction or data flow, shared or distributed memory, fine or coarse grain.

Control types include single instruction streams (including vector computers), multiple instruction streams, and networked CPUs. For the last two, static interconnect network topologies include ring, star, mesh, hypercube, complete graph, and tree. Dynamic interconnects may rely on bus or crossbar switching, or a blend. For machines and clusters or networks of machines with distributed memory, control most frequently relies on message passing. At the loosest gauge, the messaging may be over the Internet; well-known examples are the background calculations for the SETI@home project (http://setiathome.ssl.berkeley.edu/) and the search for Mersenne primes (http://www.mersenne.org/prime.htm). A tighter example is FlashMob computing (http://flashmobcomputing.org).

Real-time systems

There are unlikely to be any specific items about gate arrays, embedded systems, state-table programming, or the like. But you should appreciate the obvious differences required by real-time applications in reliability, robustness, compactness, redundancy, and validity.

Graphics

Details of video or other graphics displays can obviously be ignored, but you should be aware of several issues mediated by the displays. The first are related to digital signal processing: namely, spatial and temporal aliasing. There are many approaches to the former, including dithering and supersampling; the latter is cured by employing motion blur. The so-called functional migration cycle, or "Wheel of Reincarnation," farms processing out to peripheral hardware for efficiency, only to have that functionality later recaptured by a new generation of CPU when it appears inefficient to support two independent processors. Although not limited to graphics displays, it has a longer history and more cycles there.

Many, if not most, graphics algorithms are devoted to transformations of linear spaces of 2–4 dimensions: 2D screen coordinates, 3D model coordinates, and 4D homogeneous coordinates. The use of the constrained extra dimension in the last allows all standard CG transformations to be performed by matrix multiplication.

The NURBS (non-uniform rational B-spline) is probably the highest profile CG mathematical concept, but it is unlikely to appear on the GRE/CS.

Modeling is a hierarchy of coordinate systems. Apart from 3D output to stereo displays or rapid prototype printers, rendering is a transformation of 3D coordinate systems to 2D ones. With demands of increased photorealism come costs of space for scene storage and costs of time for processing more polygons and implementing better lighting/shadowing models and methods.

Animation is the addition of a time coordinate to the modeling process. Although rendering may need information such as whether to provide motion blur, much of the work of providing the illusion of motion over time rests in the modeling process. This movement may depend on traditional keyframing, motion capture, procedural specifications, or computed dynamics, including direct and inverse kinematics as well as physically based motion such as explosions, collisions, and falling under gravity. With the addition of time come the costs of achieving the desired illusion of motion and of computing many frames instead of a single rendered image.

Given the added demands in CG, it is little wonder that acceleration has become a strong need: faster videoboards, or display adaptors, combined with hardware support for the interpretation of OpenGL at peripheral processors. Procedural specifications reduce model size while increasing the complex realism and animation and rendering speeds.

Databases

Databases mainly take one of three forms: hierarchical, network, and relational; these are called record-based models. In addition, databases can be object-based, notably entity-relation and object-oriented models. Each has benefits and costs. But most questions concern relational databases, with the requirements and uses of normal forms heading the list. Other questions exploit the operations peculiar to relational database tables, such as join and select.

Final disclaimer

"Well, he left out _____." Even when you study every single topic in every practice exam, even if you kept every text from every undergraduate course, even if you take the exam twice, you will miss something. The point is to be prepared for the unknown as well as the known. If you can represent an integer in base 4, it will not be a shock to be asked to go to base 7. If you can trace C code, pseudoFortran will not throw you. So study, but don't go crazy trying to know it all. Doing is more than knowing, and imagination is better than regurgitation.

Chapter 5
Practice Test

Practice Test

TIME: 170 Minutes
70 Questions

DIRECTIONS: Each of the questions or incomplete statements below is followed by five suggested answers or completions. Select the one that is best in each case.

1. If the successive nodes visited during a postorder traversal of a binary tree were D B A E C F, then the tree could be represented by

(A)
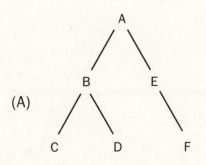

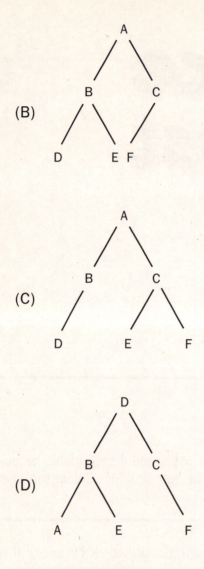

(B)

(C)

(D)

(E)   None of the above

2.   Which of the following binary tree structures would allow the fastest search for the element 2?

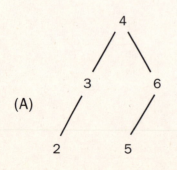

(A)

(B)

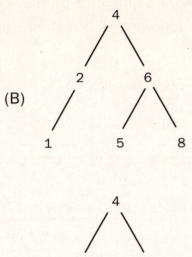

(C)

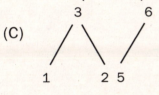

(D)

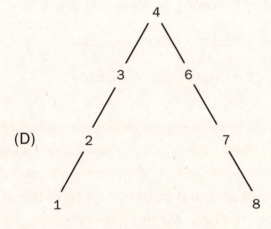

(E)   None of the above

3. Let *R* be the regular expression *(ab)* | *a* and let *S* be the regular expression *(bc)* | *c*. Which of the following is a member of the language *L(RS)*?

    (A) abbc

    (B) bca

    (C) bcab

    (D) abcc

    (E) aabc

4. Only one of the following **cannot** be represented exactly by a binary number. Which one is it?

    (A) 1/16

    (B) 327

    (C) 3.125

    (D) 0.1

    (E) 63.5

Questions 5–6 are based on the following context-free grammar.

$$<Exp> \longrightarrow <Exp> + <Exp> \ | \ <Exp> - <Exp>$$

$$<Exp> \longrightarrow <Exp> * <Exp> \ | \ <Exp> / <Exp>$$

$$<Exp> \longrightarrow <Id>$$

$$<Id> \longrightarrow a \ | \ b \ | \ \ldots \ y \ | \ z$$

5. Using best first search for a shortest path from A to Z, the order in which nodes are considered best for the path is

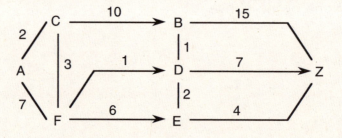

Note that these are node orders, not full paths.

(A) $A < C < F < D < E.$ (D) $A < C < D < F.$

(B) $A < C < E < B.$ (E) $A < C < B < D.$

(C) $A < C < F < E < B.$

6.   Assume the above grammar has been modified to include the additional nonterminals <Term> and <Factor>, as shown below.

<Exp> —> <Term> | <Exp> + <Term> | <Exp> – <Term>

<Term> —> <Factor> | <Term> * <Factor> | <Term> / <Factor>

<Factor> —> <Id>

<Id> —> a | b | . . . y | z

Which of these statements is true?

I.   A parse tree that corresponded with the new derivation of <EXP> would be consistent with * having a higher precedence than +.

II.   The modified grammar is unambiguous.

III.   Modifying the grammar by adding the nonterminal <Term> results in the multiplicative operator and operands, being parsed at a lower level of the parse tree than the additive operands.

(A) I only   (D) I and II only

(B) II only   (E) II and III only

(C) I, II, and III

7. A list of 500 integers is stored in order in an indexed array. To find a specific integer, what are the maximum number of searches required to perform a sequential search? To perform a binary search?

(A) 25 and 7   (D) 250 and 9

(B) 500 and 250   (E) 250 and 8

(C) 500 and 9

8.
```
#include <stdio.h>
int void main ()
{
    int j = 0, k = 0;
    f (j);
    cout << j + k;
}
void f (int& i)
{
    k = i + 3;
    i = k * i;
}
```

In the above C-like program, the **int**& *i* indicates an integer parameter called by reference. What is the value of *j* + *k* that is output by the main function?

(A) 4   (D) 3

(B) 12   (E) 1

(C) 0

9. Which of the following process dispatching policies prevent starvation?

I. First-come-first-serve (FCFS)

II. The practice of *aging* (increasing process priority with time)

III. Round-robin

(A) I only

(B) I and II only

(C) II and III only

(D) II only

(E) I, II, and III

10. It is possible to implement any combinational logic design by using NAND gates alone, or NOR gates alone. But there are still advantages to a broader set of logic gates being made available to the designer. What are they?

I. Designs that include AND, NAND, OR, NOR, and XOR gates, and inverters, can, in nearly all cases, be implemented with fewer components.

II. If the designer assumes an inclusive set of Boolean operators, the Boolean expressions used in the design process are almost always less complicated.

III. The designer is able to avoid the use of Karnaugh maps.

(A) I only

(B) II only

(C) I, II, and III

(D) I and II only

(E) None

11.

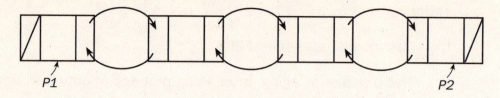

P1   P2

In the above figure $P1$ is a pointer to the first element of a doubly linked list and $P2$ is a pointer to the last element. Which of the following is true?

I.   The time required to delete the first element of the list is not dependent on the length of the list.

II.   The time required to delete the second to last element of the list is not dependent on the length of the list.

III. The insertion opertion involves the same number of steps for this list as for a singly lInked list.

(A) I and II only   (D) I, II, and III

(B) I only   (E) II and III only

(C) II only

12. Consider the transition-assigned-output-producing, deterministic finite state automaton depicted in the figure below.

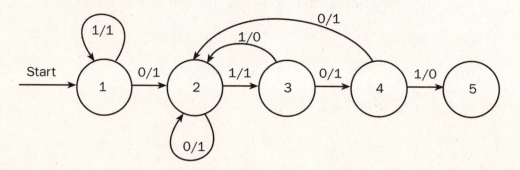

If the state on the far right is the accepting state, which of the following is **NOT** true?

(A) The input 1011101 will be accepted.

(B) The input 1011101 will be accepted and it will produce an output of 1110110.

(C) Any input ending in 101 will be accepted.

(D) There are at least two inputs that are accepted and produce 11110 as their output.

(E) The inputs 00101 and 10101 will be accepted.

13. Consider the following context-free grammar.

$$S \longrightarrow AB$$

$$A \longrightarrow 1 \mid B\,1B$$

$$B \longrightarrow 00A$$

Which of the following is a possible product?

(A) 0111

(B) 0110

(C) 1001

(D) 11011110

(E) None of the above

14. The excitation equation of a flip-flop represents the next state of its output. The excitation equation for a *JK* flip-flop is

$$\vec{Q} = \overline{J}Q + \overline{KQ}$$

Assuming Q is the output, which of the following *JK* inputs will cause the flip-flop to toggle?

(A) $J = 1, K = 1$

(D) $J = 0, K = 0$

(B) $J = 1, K = 0$

(E) None of the above

(C) $J = 0, K = 1$

15. Rigorous analysis of a particular algorithm has found that as long as the size of the input exceeds a certain constant *M*, its running time *T(n)* is, at most, proportional to the cube of the input, so that

> for all input *n* such that *n* exceeds the constant *M*,
> $T(n) \leq C * n^3$, where *C* is also a constant.

Which of these statements are true?

I.   The constants *M* and *C* are *witnesses* to the fact that *T(n)* is $O(n^3)$.

II.   For an input of a given size *n*, the algorithm's running time will be the same on any computer.

III.   If for some values of *n*, $T(n) \geq O(n^3)$, we can still say *T(n)* is $O(n^3)$, but we must find new constants *M* and *C* for those values of *n*.

(A) I only

(D) I, II, and III

(B) II only

(E) II and III only

(C) I and II only

16.

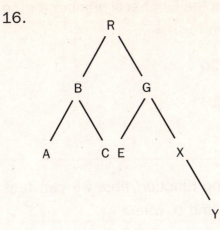

What **cannot** be said about the tree depicted above?

(A)   It is rooted.

(B)   It is a binary tree.

(C)   The height of the tree is 2.

(D)   The tree is searchable by a binary search.

(E)   It can be traversed in both preorder and postorder.

Questions 17–18 are based on the following C program fragment.

```c
int fibo (int n)
{
    if   (n < 2)
        return n;
    else
        return fibo (n-1) + fibo (n-2);
}
```

17. The above recursive function returns the Fibonacci number for the parameter n. What would *fibo* return for $n = 7$.

    (A) 8

    (B) 5

    (C) 7

    (D) 20

    (E) 13

18. To find the running time $T(n)$ for the function *fibo*, we can first assume that for some constants a and b, where

    $T(0) = T(1) = a$, and

    $T(2) = b + 2a$

    The values of $T(0)$ and $T(1)$ are based on the assumption that the **if** branch of *fibo* takes constant time a, and the value for $T(2)$ is based on the assumption that the **else** branch of *fibo* takes constant time b, plus the time for the two recursive calls. The next step is to define a recurrence relation that, if solved, would yield the running time $T(n)$ in terms of constants a and b. Which of the following is that reoccurrence relation?

    (A) $T(n) = a$ for $n > 2$

           $T(n) = b + T(n\text{-}1)$ for $n \le 2$

    (B) $T(n) = a$ for $n < 2$

           $T(n) = b + T(1) + T(2)$ for $n \ne 2$

    (C) $T(n) = a$ for $n < 1$

           $T(n) = a + b + T(n\text{-}1) + T(n{-}2)$ for $n > 2$

    (D) $T(n) = a$ for $n < 2$

           $T(n) = T(n{-}1) + a - b$ for $n \le 2$

(E) $T(n) = a$ for $n < 2$

$T(n) = b + T(n-1) + T(n-2)$ for $n \geq 2$

19. One technique used to simplify code re-defines a function with two or more parameters so that it only accepts the first parameter. However, the newly defined function returns a function that accepts the second parameter. If the original function accepted more than two parameters, the newly defined function that accepts the second parameter in turn returns a function—one that accepts the third parameter. This process continues until one of the functions returns the value that would have been returned by the original function. What term is used to refer to this technique?

(A) Top-down programming

(B) Divide and conquer

(C) Shilling

(D) The waterfall model

(E) Software engineering

20. Consider the C-like program fragment below where **mod** is the modulus operator.

```
int sum = 0;
for (i = 1; i <= 50; i++)
{
    if ((i mod 10) = 0)
        sum = sum + 1;
    else if ((i mod 15) = 0)
        sum = sum + i;
}
```

What is the value of *sum* when the loop exits?

(A) 20

(D) 65

(B) 5

(E) 120

(C) 95

21. Consider the combinational circuit below.

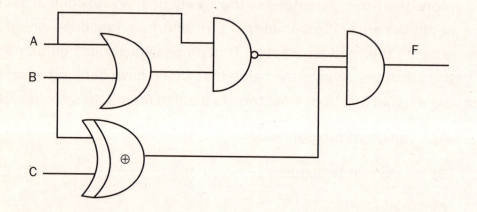

Which of the following is the Boolean representation of that circuit?

(A) $(AB \vee \overline{A}) \wedge (B \oplus C)$

(B) $(\overline{A}\,\overline{B} \vee A) \wedge (B \oplus C)$

(C) $(\overline{A}\,\overline{B} \vee \overline{A}) \wedge (B \oplus C)$

(D) $(AB \vee A) \wedge (B + C)$

(E) None of the above

22. Context-free grammars are important in the development of compilers for high-level languages. Which of the following is true about context-free grammars?

(A) The difference between context-free and context-sensitive grammars is that context-sensitive grammars allow nonterminals to be rewritten only when they appear in a certain context.

(B) The concept of context-free grammars was developed by N. Chomsky specifically for computer languages.

(C) Grammars defined by Backus-Naur Form rules are not context free.

(D) The concept of context-free grammars was originated by computer science pioneer Alan Turing.

(E) The disadvantage of context-free grammars is that the languages they define tend to be limited in their richness of functionality.

23. Fifty percent of a program will not benefit from additional processors because it is inherently sequential. If the program requires 360 seconds with only one processor, how many processors were used if the program took 240 seconds to execute? If it took 216 seconds to execute?

(A) 240 seconds: 2 processors, 216 seconds: 4 processors

(B) 240 seconds: 3 processors, 216 seconds: 5 processors

(C) 240 seconds: 2 processors, 216 seconds: 3 processors

(D) 240 seconds: 4 processors, 216 seconds: 6 processors

(E) 240 seconds: 3 processors, 216 seconds: 4 processors

24. Consider the following table of minterms and the Boolean function f(A, B, C).

Table of Three Input Minterms		
Row	**ABC**	**Minterms**
0	000	$\overline{A}\,\overline{B}\,\overline{C}$
1	001	$\overline{A}\,\overline{B}\,C$
2	010	$\overline{A}\,B\,\overline{C}$
3	011	$\overline{A}\,B\,C$
4	100	$A\,\overline{B}\,\overline{C}$
5	101	$A\,\overline{B}\,C$
6	110	$A\,B\,\overline{C}$
7	111	$A\,B\,C$

$$f(A, B, C) = m_3 + m_4 + m_5$$

What Boolean expression in terms of the A, B, C inputs of a combinational circuit is equivalent to the minterm expansion above?

(A) $f(A, B, C) = \overline{A}BC + A\overline{B}\,\overline{C} + \overline{A}B\overline{C}$

(B) $f(A, B, C) = AB + BC + AC$

(C) $f(A, B, C) = \overline{A}BC + A\overline{B}\,\overline{C} + A\overline{B}C$

(D) $f(A, B, C) = AB\overline{C} + A\overline{B}C + \overline{A}BC$

(E) $f(A, B, C) = (A + B + \overline{C}) \wedge (\overline{A} + B + C)$

25. If *letter* is any member of the alphabet, and *digit* is any Arabic numeral, then the regular expression

identifier = letter (letter letter | letter digit | digit letter | digit digit)

represents the set of all three character alphanumeric identifiers that begin with a letter. Which of the following regular expressions represent all odd-numbered alphanumeric words that begin with a letter?

(A) *letter | (letter | digit)*

(B) *letter (letter | digit)**

(C) *letter* (letter letter | letter digit | digit letter | digit digit)*

(D) *letter (letter letter | letter digit | digit letter | digit digit)**

(E) *letter | (letter | digit)$^+$*

26. When dynamic scoping is used, identifiers not declared within a subprogram are associated with an identifier of the same name currently recognized by the calling code. This association takes place at execution time. When static scoping is used, non-local identifiers are associated, at compile time, with an identifier of the same name declared within an enclosing subprogram, or program.

```
program main (input, output);
    var i, j: integer;
    procedure A;
        begin
            if i > j then i := 2 * i
            else j := 2 * j
        end;
    procedure B;
        var i, j;
        begin
            i := 1;
            j := 2;
            A
        end;
    begin
        i := 25;
        j := 35;
        B;
        write (j);
    end;
```

What is the value of *j* output by the above Pascal-like program, if dynamic scoping is in effect? If static scoping is in effect?

(A)   dynamic: 70, static: 35

(B)   dynamic: 70, static: 4

(C)   dynamic: 35, static: 70

(D)   dynamic: 4, static: 70

(E)   The value of *j* will not be output due to a run-time error.

27.   Consider the following type, structure, and pointer to a structure, which are defined and declared in C language.

```
int sum = 0;
typedef cell CellPtr*;
struct cell {
    float floatNbr;
    CellPtr next_cell; }
CellPtr X;
```

Assume that the above code is used to implement a linked list, and that *X* points to a cell before a cell that is to be deleted. Which of these statements correctly deletes the cell from the list?

(A) *X->nextCell = X->nextCell->nextCell;*

(B) *X = X->nextCell;*

(C) *X = X->nextCell->nextCell;*

(D) *X->nextCell = X->cellPtr->nextCell;*

(E) *X->cellPtr = X->cellPtr->nextCell;*

Questions 28–30 refer to the following diagram of a decoder.

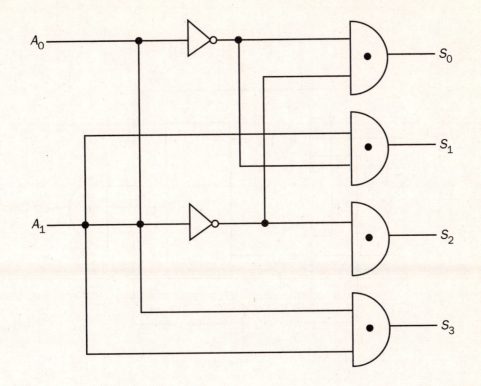

28. Assume the delay of the AND gates is 20 ns, and the delay of the inverters is 12 ns. What would be the delay from the time the A^n inputs appear until there is a valid selection of one of the S^n lines?

    (A) 32 ns   (D) 104 ns

    (B) 20 ns   (E) 12 ns

    (C) 94 ns

29. This question refers both to the decoder and the memory cell depicted below.

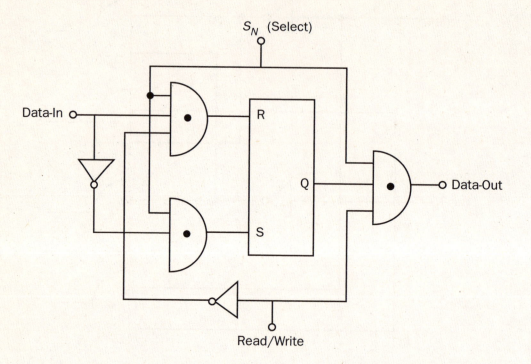

Assume one of the S^n lines of the decoder goes into the SELECT line of the memory cell. And assume, again, the delay of the AND gates is 20 ns, and the inverters is 12 ns. What is the delay from the time the address, A^n, is first input into the *decoder* until the data stored in the *memory cell* first appears at the DATA-OUT output? (Assume READ/WRITE goes high simultaneously with address A^n.)

(A)   84 ns

(D)   144 ns

(B)   72 ns

(E)   52 ns

(C)   64 ns

30. What is the total WRITE time of the memory if the transition time of the memory cell's RS flip-flops is 20 ns. (Assume READ/WRITE goes low and DATA-IN assumes its value simultaneously with address A^n.)

    (A) 92 ns

    (B) 72 ns

    (C) 104 ns

    (D) 84 ns

    (E) 64 ns

31. The first four levels of the OSI Reference Model appear below on the left, and the TCP/IP protocol suite equivalents appear below on the right, except for layer two.

Transport Layer	Transport Control Protocol (TCP)
Network Layer	Internet Protocol (IP)
Data Link Layer	_____
Physical Layer	Physical Medium

    Which of the following protocols is used by TCP/IP to transport IP packets across the physical medium, and as such, corresponds closely to the Data Link Layer of the OSI Reference Model?

    (A) Asynchronous Transfer Mode (ATM)

    (B) Frame Relay

    (C) Ethernet

    (D) Token Ring

    (E) All of the above

32. The binary equivalent of 4,765,838,193 is

    1 0001 1100 0001 0000 1110 1011 0111 0001.

    What is the hexadecimal equivalent?

    (A) 17C13EB71

    (B) 11B10DB71

    (C) 11C10EB71

    (D) 1FC10EB75

    (E) 1CFEDB44

Questions 33–35 refer to the Pascal-like code fragment below.

```
            ptr end_Q
        record (... ptr next ...)
        cobegin
          repeat handle_pg_faults;
          repeat supervise_IO_reqs;
        coend
procedure handle_page_faults        procedure super_IO_req
begin                               begin
  end_Q^next <- Adr (pg_fault)        end_Q^next <- Adr (IO_req)
  end_Q <- Adr (pg_fault)             end_Q <- Adr (IO_req)
end                                 end
```

33. Two independent processes append to a shared queue, as shown in the above concurrent program fragment. The first concurrent procedure, *handle_page_faults,* queues processes blocked due to page faults; the second concurrent procedure, *super_IO_req,*

queues processes blocked due to input/output requests. What is wrong with the above approach?

I. The page fault handler and the input/output supervisor are not synchronized with each other.

II. There is no mechanism such as WAIT or SIGNAL to allow communication between the two parallel procedures.

III. It is possible for either the page fault handler or the input/output supervisor to be interrupted in the middle of the queuing operation, resulting in a pointer error, which could be catastrophic.

(A) I only

(B) III only

(C) I and II only

(D) I, II, and III

(E) II and III only

34. Consider the following modified procedures to queue processes blocked due to page fault, or I/O request.

```
procedure handle_page_faults        procedure super_IO_req
begin                                begin
  loop until TS (s);                   loop until TS (s);
    end_Q^next <- Adr (pg_fault)          end_Q^next <- Adr (IO_req)
    end_Q <- Adr (pg_fault)               end_Q <- Adr (IO_req)
  s = true                             s = true
end                                  end
```

The above procedures now have test and a set instruction that tests a flag, s. If s is raised, both procedures lower it in one uninterruptable instruction TS (s). Once the flag has been lowered (to prevent being interrupted during a queuing operation), both procedures append a process to the queue. Then they raise the flag (set *s* to **true**). What, if anything, is less than optimal about the above approach?

(A) The the page fault handler and the I/O supervisor are still not synchronized.

(B) The test and set instruction, *TS (s)*, is not positioned just prior to the critical sections of these two competing procedures.

(C) The procedures loop on both the test and set instruction, tying up valuable processor time.

(D) There is still no communication in the form of a WAIT or a SIGNAL operation between the two concurrent procedures.

(E) It is not necessary to set the flag, *s*, to true at the end of the critical section.

35. Consider the further modification of the procedures that append processes to a shared queue, as shown below.

```
procedure handle_page_faults            procedure super_IO_req
begin                                    begin
  P(s)                                     P(s)
    end_Q^next <- Adr (pg_fault)            end_Q^next <- Adr (IO_req)
    end_Q <- Adr (pg_fault)                 end_Q <- Adr (IO_req)
  V(s)                                     V(s)
end                                      end
```

The above procedures now have a **P** operation, which allows a process to test a semaphore, *s*, and then to either enter a critical section of code, or to become blocked until it is all right to enter that section. Also, the **V** operation to raise the semaphore has been added. Which statements are true about the above approach?

I. The **P** operation turns the process over to the operating system, which may block it and dispatch a ready process to optimally utilize the resources allocated to that process such as its processor.

II. When the semaphore is true again, the operating system will cause a process blocked on that semaphore to run again, executing code immediately following its **P** operation.

III. The page fault handler and input/output supervisor don't need to communicate with each other, because they are independent processes that just happen to have critical sections of code that access the same queue.

(A) I only

(B) II only

(C) I and II only

(D) I, II, and III

(E) II and III only

36. Assume the following:

1. a computer password is 9 characters in length;
2. the program that checks its validity is case insensitive;
3. the password may consist of alphanumeric characters (a–z and 0–9) except for the first character, which must be a letter;
4. the underscore character is considered a letter.

How many possible passwords are there?

(A) 9^{26}

(B) $27 * 37^8$

(C) $26 * 8^{26}$

(D) $26 * 37^8$

(E) 37^9

Questions 37–38 are based on the following automaton.

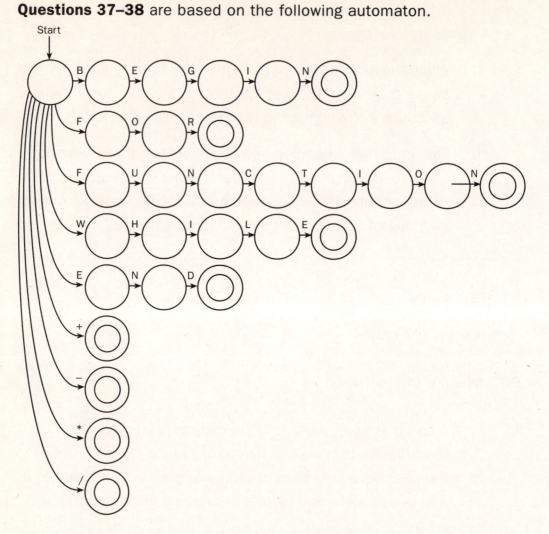

37. The above finite state automaton was designed to be capable of recognizing all the tokens of a simple computer language. What are the tokens of that langauge?

   (A)   **for, while, begin, end**, and **function**

   (B)   +, −, *, /

   (C)   **for, while, begin, end, function**, +, −, *, / and =

   (D)   It is not known because the above automaton is not deterministic.

   (E)   **while, begin, end, function**, +, −, *, / and =

38. Which of these statements is true about the above finite state automaton?

    (A) It is deterministic in the case of **for**.

    (B) It can be modified so that it is deterministic and still accepts the same input.

    (C) It is not deterministic in the case of **while**.

    (D) The disadvantage of this type of automaton (whether deterministic or not) is that it can't easily be converted to code.

    (E) It is not deterministic in the case of **begin.**

39. Vector processors are considered a good match for matrix multiplication. Why is that?

    I.   Due to the nature of computer multiplication, it takes a lot of steps to multiply two binary numbers; but a vector processor, once its pipeline is full, can kick out a multiplicative result on almost every clock cycle.

    II. Vector processors have analog components, which tend to increase computational speed.

    III. Matrices have components that can be multiplied in parallel, taking full advantage of the vector processor's parallel capabilities.

    IV. Matrices allow the vector processor to ignore the sign bit, thereby saving steps in the computational process.

    (A) I only   (D) I, II, and III

    (B) II only   (E) IV

    (C) I and III only

40. Compute the frame check sequence (CRC for Ethernet frames) from the following message polynomial G(x) and generating polynomial P(x):

    $G(x) = x^7 + x^4 + x^3 + x^2 + x^1 + x^0$ OR 10011111

    $P(x) = x^5 + x^4 + x^2 + x^0$ OR 110101

    (A) 10011   (D) 10101

    (B) 11001   (E) 10001

    (C) 11110

41. Consider the following diagram of a complementary metal oxide (CMOS) inverter.

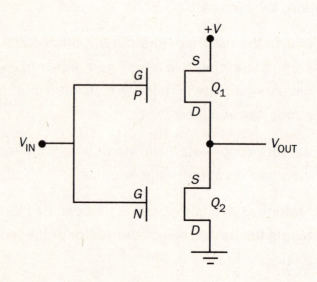

    Which of the following has played a role in the current popularity of CMOS in today's computers?

    (A) It has faster switching speeds than rival technologies: transistor-transistor logic (TTL), and emitter coupled logic (ECL).

(B) CMOS makes it unnecessary to dope the semi-conductor (silicon) with p-material or n-material.

(C) CMOS devices avoid the use of costly transistors.

(D) CMOS has extremely low power consumption, avoiding the myriad of problems associated with overheating and cooling of electronic components.

(E) The simplicity of its structure makes CMOS easy to design.

42. What is the primary advantage of dynamic RAM (DRAM) versus static RAM (SRAM)?

(A) It is much less expensive.

(B) The data in DRAM is not lost when the power is turned off.

(C) DRAM has much faster access speeds compared to SRAM.

(D) SRAM looses its data on every read, so that it must immediately be written back, which increases the total access time.

(E) The requirement that DRAM be refreshed periodically is really its greatest asset, because of the increased stability of the system.

43. A register transfer language is defined as follows,

$$XY: bus \longleftarrow R^n, \ WZ: R^n \longleftarrow bus$$

where *XY* and *WZ* represent the respective inputs of a multiplexer and decoder. These two devices are utilized to select and decode the source and destination registers of a four-register bus system.

The inputs that select (or decode) the registers are designated as follows:

MUX Inputs	Decoder Inputs	Register Selected or Decoded
00	01	R^1
01	10	R^2
10	11	R^3
11	00	R^4

Assume an input variable is a one unless otherwise designated (e.g., YZ' = 10). Which of the following statements represent a data transfer from R^3 to R^4, given appropriate input?

(A) XY': bus <— R^4, $W'Z'$: R^3 <— bus

(B) XY': bus <— R^3, WZ: R^4 <— bus

(C) XY': bus <— R^3, $W'Z'$: R^4 <— bus

(D) $X'Y'$: bus <— R^3, WZ': R^4 <— bus

(E) $X\overline{Y}'$: bus <— R^2, $\overline{YZ}$: R^1 <— bus

44.   The control unit (CU) of a particular CPU has four basic micro-programs, or cycles, that form the basis for executing all of its machine code instructions. These cycles are shown below.

   C^0 Fetch cycle (input instruction from RAM)

   C^1 Indirect cycle (input address of operand)

   C^2 Interrupt cycle (service I/O or other request)

   C^3 Execute cycle (carryout instruction)

The inputs into the logic portion of the CU are designated by C^nT^n, where the timing variable T^n selects the individual micro-operations of the cycle.

The CPU registers pertinent to these basic cycles are as follows:

PC: Program Counter

MBR: Memory Buffer Register

MAR: Memory Address Register

IR: Instruction Register

Assume that for this control unit, if an interrupt occurs, the interrupt cycle, C^2, follows the fetch cycle, C^0 given below. At what individual micro-operation does the interrupt cycle take a wrong turn?

C^0T^0 : MAR <— PC   Instruction address is in *PC*

C^0T^1 : PC <— PC + 1   Increment program counter

C^0T^2 : MBR <— M [MAR]   Get instruction from RAM

C^0T^3 : IR <— MBR   Instruction register gets instruction

I. C^2T^0 : PC <— I_adr.   *PC* gets interrupt address

II. C^2T^1 : MAR <— PC   Interrupt instruction adr. is in *PC*

III. C^2T^2 : PC <— PC + 1   Increment program counter

IV. C^2T^3 : MBR <— M [MAR]   Get instruction from RAM

(A)   I

(B)   II

(C)   III

(D)   IV

(E)   None

45. The symbol table created by the compiler of a computer language relies on the following hash function,

$$H(n) = (I^0 \text{ XOR } I^1) \text{ XOR } I^2) \dots \text{ XOR } I^n) \bmod m)$$

where an identifier is comprised of characters I^0 through I^n.

The characters that make up the identifiers of this language are represented by ASCII values, and take one byte of storage. The data structure that is used to store the symbol table is an array with a maximum size of $m = 10$. Collisions are resolved by rehashing as follows,

$$RH\ (n,\ k) = ((k * H\ (n))\ \bmod m) \qquad \text{where}$$

$k =$ the number of collisions + 1.

If the identifier *A1* (ASCII A = 74 and ASCII 1 = 49) is to be added to the symbol table, and only the slots indexed by 3 and 6 are occupied, which of the following is the rehash function value that will ultimately resolve the collision?

(A) $RH\ (A1,\ 1) = ((1 * H\ (A1))\ \bmod 10) = 6$

(B) $RH\ (A1,\ 1) = ((1 * H\ (A1))\ \bmod 10) = 7$

(C) $RH\ (A1,\ 3) = ((3 * H\ (A1))\ \bmod 10) = 4$

(D) $RH\ (A1,\ 3) = ((3 * H\ (A1))\ \bmod 10) = 9$

(E) $RH\ (A1,\ 2) = ((2 * H\ (A1))\ \bmod 10) = 25$

46. A particular implementation of demand paging relies upon three hardware registers: (1) the **page table register**, which holds the beginning address of the page table in main storage, (2) the **page register**, which holds the high-order bits (the page number) of the virtual memory location for that page, and (3) the **index register**,

which holds the low-order bits, or the index within that page. The page table below flags (1 = present in memory) and provides the number of the page frame.

		Page
Addr.	Flag	Frame
...		
0410	0	—
0411	1	17
0412	1	21
0413	1	03

page table register = 400
page register = 11
index register = 312

Assuming the above values of the **page table register**, the **page register**, the **index register**, and that one page consists of 1,024 words, and also that the address of the first page frame (frame 00) is 2,000, what is the storage location being referenced?

(A) 4111

(B) 18032

(C) 19408

(D) 19720

(E) The page is not currently resident in memory, so a page fault would have to be serviced before its location could be computed.

47. How would the following expression be represented in prefix notation?

$(a * b + c * d) / ((e + f) * g)$

(A) $ab*cd*+ef+g*/$

(B) $/+*ab*cd*+efg$

(C) $+*ab*cd/*+efg$

(D) $+*ab*cd*+efg/$

(E) None of the above

48. There are three fundamental policies that deal with the problem of deadlock: (1) *prevention*, (2) *avoidance*, and (3) *detection and recovery*. Which of these statements, regarding the policy of avoidance, is true?

I.   If the sequence of requests for resource allocation is known for each concurrently executing process, deadlock can be avoided.

II. The *circular wait condition*, necessary for deadlock to occur, can be suppressed by *hierarchic allocation*.

III. If the sequence of each concurrently executing processes requests for resource allocation is not known, but their total demand is, deadlock can be avoided by what is known as the *banker's algorithm*.

(A) I and III only

(B) II only

(C) I, II, and III

(D) III only

(E) II and III only

49. Consider the following Pascal-like concurrent program fragment.

```
        buffer_array record
        semaphore initiate, finish
        initiate <- 0
        finish <- 1
        cobegin
          repeat producer;
          repeat consumer;
        coend
procedure producer              procedure consumer
begin                           begin
  produce record                  P (initiate)
  P (finish)                      read record from array
  write record into array         V (finish)
  V (initiate)                    consume record
end                             end
```

Which statement is true regarding the two concurrent, cooperating procedures: *producer* and *consumer*?

(A) The *producer* and *consumer* are not synchronized.

(B) Valuable processor time is wasted in both of the above parallel procedures while they wait on the **P** and **V** operations.

(C) There is communication between processes as the **P** and **V** operation provide the functionality of WAIT and SIGNAL.

(D) Since there are a number of producers and consumers, the binary semaphore *finish* should have been initialized to more than 1.

(E) The problem of a possible read by the *consumer* of an empty buffer has not been alleviated.

50. Since disk space must be allocated dynamically, there must be an efficient system of allocating and keeping track of physical blocks of storage on hard disks. Which of the following statements are true about the three most common methods used to organize secondary storage into files?

    (A) A file can be created and maintained by linking together a chain of fixed sized blocks (the *block chain* method), but a file descriptor must be included in each block.

    (B) The *index* method transfers the pointers to a single block, allowing much faster access to individual file records, but unfortunately the tradeoff is increased complexity.

    (C) One of the disadvantages of the *block chain* method is that once a file is created from a large block of free disk space, future growth of the file is restricted in order fot it to remain within that block.

    (D) A *file map* can be created that links words in the *file map* in a one-to-one correspondence with file blocks; however, the access time is no faster than the *block chain* method.

    (E) Most file management systems avoid using the same block size for all types of files.

Questions 51 and 52 refer to the following figure.

$$x^5(x^7 + x^4 + x^3 + x^2 + x^1 + x^0) = x^{12} + x^9 + x^8 + x^7 + x^6 + x^5$$

$$= 1001111100000$$

51. There is a STA (store the contents of register A) instruction in the instruction set for the CPU above. The instruction format and an example STA instruction are shown below.

	0 3	4 15
	OPC	Address
STA	0001	101101110010

The first 4 bits identify the opcode (OPC), and the last 12 bits identify the address.

Assume the inputs into the logic portion of the CU are designated by $C^n T^n$, where C^n identifies the cycle and the timing variable, T^n identifies the step.

Further assume the fetch cycle C^0 followed by the execute cycle C^1 for a STA instruction takes place as follows:

$C^0 T^0$: MAR <— PC   Instruction address is in *PC*

$C^0 T^1$: MBR <— M [MAR]   Get instruction from RAM

$C^0 T^2$: PC <— PC + 1   Increment program counter

$C^0 T^3$: IR <— MBR   Instruction register gets instruction

$C^1 T^0$: MAR <— IR(4–15)   MAR gets address to store the A register

$C^1 T^1$: MBR <— A   Memory buffer register gets A

$C^1 T^2$: M [MAR]<— MBR   Contents of A are stored in RAM

What is the decimal equivalent of the address where the A register would be stored by the example STA instruction?

(A) 6578

(B) 4072

(C) 2930

(D) 119

(E) 12774

52. Assume there is a STAX instruction that adds the address portion to the X register, then stores the A register at that address. The instruction format, an example STAX instruction, and the contents of the X register are shown below.

```
         0   3    4              15
             OPC      Address
STAX         0011     101101110010
             0                15
X register   0001101101110010
```

What is the decimal equivalent of the address where the A register would be stored in memory?

(A) 1230   (D) 34105

(B) 6458   (E) 9956

(C) 7026

53. The definition of the dot product of two vectors **u** and **v** is as follows:

$$\mathbf{u} \bullet \mathbf{v} = \mathbf{u}_1 \mathbf{v}_1 + \mathbf{u}_2 \mathbf{v}_2 + \dots + \mathbf{u}_n \mathbf{v}_n$$

Why is the dot product also called the scalar product of **u** and **v**?

(A) It allows the vectors to be represented in multi-dimensional space.

(B) The dot product provides a way of obtaining a leading 1 when performing Gauss-Jordan elimination, thus scaling back the required number of steps.

(C) It provides a measure of the length of the vector.

(D) A dot product has magnitude and sign, but not direction.

(E) None of the above.

54. A form of cabling that consists of an inner and outer conductor that are separated by an insulator, but share a common axis is called *coaxial cable* or *coax*. It was quite common in early local area networks, and is still often used for high-speed Internet access. What is the advantage of coax versus other forms of cabling?

    (A) The electrical characteristics of coax make it unusually tolerant of background noise and interference.

    (B) It is more flexible than its chief rival, twisted pair.

    (C) It is capable of broadband transmission.

    (D) Coaxial cable does not require repeaters, unlike fiber optic cable and twisted pair.

    (E) The popularity of ADSL has given coax a new lease on life.

55. A 1024 byte cache memory can be characterized by the following data,

hit time	4 clock cycles
transfer rate	2 bytes per clock cycle
miss rate	cache size in bytes / (block size in bytes * 128)
block size	32 to 512 bytes

    and by these formulas:

access time	4 clock cycles
miss penalty	access time + block size / transfer rate

The above access time refers to the additional, or latency, time required to access noncache memory. The formula for average memory access time (AMAT) is given by:

AMAT = hit time + miss rate * miss penalty

Which of the following is the best choice for block size?

(A) 32 bytes   (D) 256 bytes

(B) 64 bytes   (E) 512 bytes

(C) 128 bytes

56. Compilers of block-structured languages, such as Pascal, and recursive languages, such as C, create object code for the purpose of maintaining an activation stack during run-time. The activation stack holds dynamically-created records pertaining to each currently active procedure and function. Which of the following variables would actually be found in one of these activation records?

(A) The individual cells of a linked list that has been declared and created by a function or procedure

(B) The components of a dynamically allocated array, locally declared by a function or procedure

(C) Global variables in the case of C language

(D) The pointer to the previous activation record on the stack

(E) The stack pointer

57. If the names and locations of files on a disk are maintained in a linear table, a large catalog is difficult to update, because sections nearly as long as the whole table have to be shifted to insert and delete new or old entries. Some systems utilize a hash table,

which is an extremely fast and efficient method of maintaining large tables of information; however, most systems rely on a tree structure to organize and store disk files.

Which of these statements is true about tree-structured file systems?

I.   A directory tree structure is inherently user friendly.

II. Since it is important that each file has a globally unique name, a tree directory structure is convenient, because the globally unique name is always the path to the file concatenated with the file name.

III. One of the advantages of relying on a tree structure for file organization is that the disk becomes less fragmented over time.

A) I and II only   (D) III only

(B) II only   (E) II and III only

(C) I, II, and III

58. If the following expression was evaluated in postfix using a push down stack,

$(a * b + c * d) / ((e + f) * g)$

where $a = 1, b = 2, c = 10, d = 7, e = 3, f = 9,$ and $g = 12$

what would be the first ten stack operations?

(A) PUSH (a), PUSH (b), POP, POP, PUSH (2),
     PUSH (c), PUSH (d), POP, POP, PUSH (70)

(B) PUSH (a), PUSH (b), PUSH (c), POP, POP,
     PUSH (20), POP, POP, PUSH (20), PUSH (d)

(C)   PUSH (e), PUSH (f), POP, PUSH (12), POP,
PUSH (g), POP, PUSH (144), PUSH (d), POP

(D)   PUSH (g), PUSH (e), PUSH (+), POP, POP,
PUSH (f), POP, POP, PUSH (*), PUSH (d)

(E)   PUSH (a), PUSH (b), PUSH (+), POP, POP,
PUSH (3), POP, POP, PUSH (17), PUSH (/)

59.   Which of the graphs shown below is nonplanar?

I.

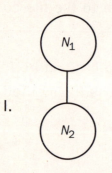

II.

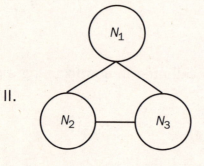

III.

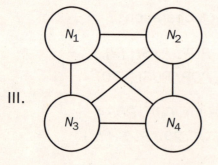

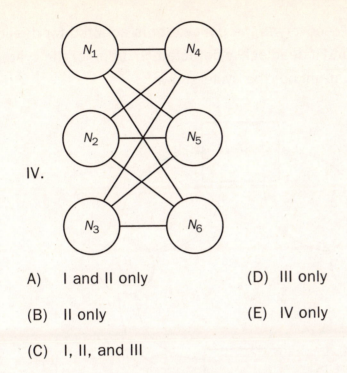

IV.

A) I and II only

(B) II only

(C) I, II, and III

(D) III only

(E) IV only

60. Sockets were developed for the Berkeley Software Distribution (BSD) version of the UNIX operating system to communicate using the TCP/IP Internet protocol. Which of these statements regarding the address of BSD sockets is valid?

I.   The first part of the address is a 16 bit integer identifying the **protocol family**.

II. The second part of the address is a 16-bit integer which identifies the **port number** assigned to the process.

III. The third part is a 32 bit integer, the **IP address** that is used to logically identify a device on an IP (Internet Protocol) network.

(A) I and II only

(B) II only

(C) III only

(D) I, II, and III

(E) None

61. If detection and recovery is the policy that is adopted for dealing with deadlock, and if deadlock is detected, in order for the system to recover it must unknot the cycle shown.

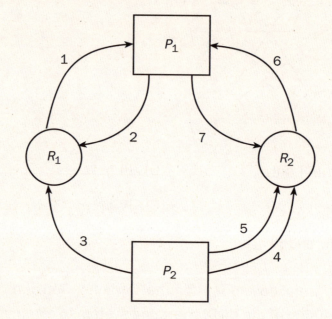

What steps would unknot the cycle?

(A) Remove edges 1, 4, and 7.

(B) Remove edges 2, 3, and 5.

(C) Remove edges 1, 4, and 5.

(D) Remove edges 1 and 3.

(E) Remove edges 1 and 7.

62. Consider the following C-like program fragment.

```
typedef struct NODE *nbrList;
struct NODE {
    int item;
    nbrList next; };
nbrList MergeNbrList (nbrList list1, nbrList
list2)
{
    if (list1 == NULL) return list2;
    else if (list2 == NULL) return list1;
    else if (list1->item <= list2->item)
    {
        list1->next = merge (list1->next,
list2)
        return list1;
    }
    else
    {
        list2->next = merge (list2->next,
list1)
        return list2;
    }
}
```

What is being merged by the above function *MergeNbrList*?

(A) Two lists of items

(B) Two lists of numbers

(C) Two lists of integers

(D) Two linked lists of records (**struct** in C language) that are ordered by the numerical value of the *item* field, which is declared as an integer.

(E) Two linked lists of records

Questions **63–65** are based on the following C-like program fragment.

```
typedef struct cell *Nodes;
struct cell {
    int Nodename;
    Nodes next;
};
enum CheckType {Seen, Unseen};
typedef struct {
    enum CheckType Check;
    Nodes descendants;
} Graph[LIMIT];
```

63. The above type definitions and variable declarations set up the data structure needed to implement an undirected graph. Which of the following are variables that identify the individual nodes of the graph?

    I.   *Nodename*

    II. *Nodes*

    III. *Graph [index]* where *index* is an **int** <= *LIMIT*

    (A) I only

    (B) I and II only

    (C) II only

    (D) I, II, and III

    (E) None

64. Consider the C-like function that searches the *a* graph structure created from the above type definitions and variable declarations.

```
void depth (int index, Graph g)
{
    Nodes ptr;
    int v;
    g[index].Check = Seen;
```

```
        ptr = g[index].descendants;
        while (ptr != NULL) {
            v := ptr->Nodename;
            if (g[index].Check == Unseen) depth
    (v, g);
            ptr = ptr->next;
        }
    }
```

The function *depth* performs a depth-first search of the graph it receives in the form of the parameter *g*. What could be said about the function *depth*?

(A)   The function doesn't accomplish anything, because it has a void return value.

(B)   It visits most of the nodes of *g*, and marks them as *seen*.

(C)   It creates a tree structure out of the part of the graph it searches by identifying some, but not necessarily all, of the descendants of each node.

(D)   It computes the depth of each node.

(E)   None of the above.

65.   Consider the C-like program fragment below.

```
    void depthFrst (Graph g);
    {
        int index;
        for (index = 0; index < LIMIT; index++)
            g[index].Check = Unseen;
        for (index = 0; index < LIMIT; index++)
            if (g[index].Check == Unseen) depth
    (index, g);
    }
```

The function *depthFrst* creates a forest of trees that provide complete information about the undirected graph. Let m equal the number of nodes of the graph, let l equal the number of arcs, and let n equal the greater of the two values of l and m: then the running time, $T(n)$, of the entire algorithm can be given by the following:

(A) $T(n) = O(n^2)$

(B) $T(n) = O(2n)$

(C) $T(n) = O(n/2)$

(D) $T(n) = O(n^3)$

(E) $T(n) = O(n)$

66. In logic programming there are two types of propositional literals: positive propositional literals (propositional variables), and negative propositional literals (negations of propositional variables). A propositional clause can be formed by connecting propositional literals with the v operator. There is a special propositional clause called the Horn clause that includes at most one positive propositional literal. Which of the following are examples of Horn clauses:

I. $\{p^1, \neg\, p^2\}\, \{p^3\}\, \{q\}$

II. $\{p^1, \neg\, p^2\}\, \{p^3\}$

III. $\{q\}$

IV. $\{p^1\}\, \{p^2\}\, \{q\}$

(A)   I only   (D)   I, II, and III

(B)   I and II only   (E)   I, III, and IV

(C)   II only

67. Consider the current state of a queue, as shown below.

    Queue {C, B, F, G}

    Assume that after six operations are performed on the queue, the state of the queue is now as follows:

    Queue {F, G, I, A, D, H}

    Which operations were performed?

    (A) enqueue (I), enqueue (A), dequeue, dequeue, enqueue (H), dequeue

    (B) enqueue (I), dequeue, dequeue, enqueue (A), enqueue (D), dequeue

    (C) enqueue (I), enqueue (A), dequeue, enqueue (D), enqueue (H), dequeue

    (D) enqueue (G), enqueue (I), dequeue, enqueue (D), enqueue (H), dequeue

    (E) enqueue (A), enqueue (B), dequeue, enqueue (F), enqueue (G), dequeue

68. Consider the deterministic finite automaton below.

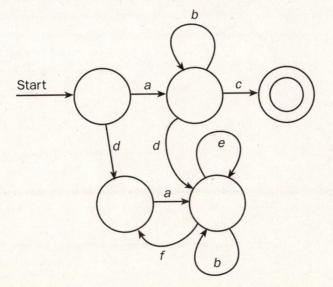

Which regular expression is equivalent to the set of strings accepted by the automaton?

(A)   ab* + c

(B)   a + b* c

(C)   ab + c*

(D)   a*b + (b + c)

(E)   ab + b*c

69. (a)

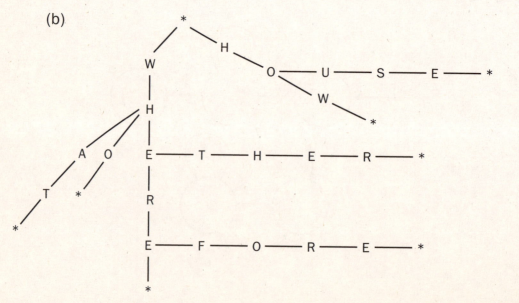

(b)

A trie is a specialized tree that is used to efficiently represent character strings. The root node and the leaf nodes are designated by the asterisk. The trie above represents these words:

who   how

what

where

If the trie were expanded to include: "whether," "wherefore," and "house," how many nodes would be required to form the trie?

(A) 24

(D) 23

(B) 30

(E) 19

(C) 16

70. Define a relation R as follows: if $x \bmod n$ equals $y \bmod n$, then $x R y$. The relation R is represented as:

$$x \equiv y \quad \bmod n$$

Which of the properties of an equivalence relation does R have?

I.   Reflexivity

II.   Symmetry

III. Transitivity

(A) I only

(D) II, and III only

(B) I and II only

(E) I, II, and III

(C) II only

Answer Key

1.	(C)	25.	(D)	48.	(A)
2.	(B)	26.	(C)	49.	(C)
3.	(A)	27.	(A)	50.	(B)
4.	(D)	28.	(A)	51.	(C)
5.	(A)	29.	(B)	52.	(E)
6.	(C)	30.	(B)	53.	(D)
7.	(C)	31.	(E)	54.	(A)
8.	(D)	32.	(C)	55.	(E)
9.	(E)	33.	(B)	56.	(D)
10.	(D)	34.	(C)	57.	(A)
11.	(A)	35.	(D)	58.	(A)
12.	(C)	36.	(B)	59.	(E)
13.	(C)	37.	(C)	60.	(D)
14.	(A)	38.	(B)	61.	(E)
15.	(A)	39.	(C)	62.	(D)
16.	(D)	40.	(C)	63.	(A)
17.	(C)	41.	(D)	64.	(C)
18.	(E)	42.	(A)	65.	(E)
19.	(C)	43.	(C)	66.	(D)
20.	(B)	44.	(A)	67.	(C)
21.	(B)	45.	(D)	68.	(E)
22.	(A)	46.	(D)	69.	(B)
23.	(B)	47.	(B)	70.	(E)
24.	(C)				

Detailed Explanations of Answers

1. **C**

In the case of the tree shown in answer (C), once the left-most tree has been traversed twice, we have reached the leaf D. From there we visit the root, B, and since there is no right-most tree, we again visit the root of the subtree or tree, A. Next, we traverse the right-most tree in postorder, twice, and reach the leaf E, from there we visit the root, C, and traverse the right-most tree in postorder by visiting the last unvisited node, F. So (C) is the correct answer.

2. **B**

This answer is easy. No matter what search method is used, the depth from the root node to the element 2 is the least in the tree depicted in answer (B), so that will be the fastest.

3. **A**

The language *L(R)* of a regular expression is the set of all strings (elements) that a regular expression represents. In the case of the regular expression *R*, there are two elements: *ab* and *a*. Likewise, the regular expression *S* represents two possible strings: *bc* and *c*. The language *L(RS)* of the regular expression *RS* consists of all the strings represented by all possible concatenations *rs* such that *r* is an element of *R* and *s* is an element of *S*. Answers (B) and (C) begin with an element of S, so the concantenation is not in the right order. Answer (D) includes a nonelement of either regular expression: *cc*, and (E) likewise: *aa*. (A), however, is made up of an element of *R*, *ab*, and followed by an element of *S*, *bc*, so (A) is the correct anwer.

4. **D**

Any fraction whose denominator is a power of two can be represented exactly by a binary number, and since 16 is a power of two, (A) can be ruled out. Another good rule of thumb is that any integer can be represented exactly in binary, so (B) can also be ruled out. Since the part of (C) that comes after the decimal point is equivalent to 1/8 (8 is a power of 2) and the part that comes before the decimal point is an integer, (C) is the sum of two numbers that can be represented in binary, and thus can be eliminated. Likewise, (E) is part fraction (the denominator is a power of 2) and part integer. That leaves (D) as the only possible answer.

5. **A**

Best first is greedy in that it immediately chooses the most profitable of alternatives. Start at *A*, choose *AC* (shorter than *AF*), choose *C* to *F* (since 5 is shorter than 7), choose *FD* (produces a shorter path than *ACB* or *AFE*), choose *DB* (total path cost = 7). Now the *B* path stops because 15 is more expensive than the *DE* alternative (*A..D* = 8). Finally, *EZ* is chosen. The node ordering of Choice (B) is wrong since *E* precedes *B*. Likewise, choice (C) assumes the same. Choice (D) assumes path *ABCD* for *D* to precede *F* (nonoptimal *CB* or *DB* decision). Choice (E) makes a nonoptimal decision favoring *CB*.

6. **C**

The addition of the nonterminals *<Term>* and *<Factor>* results in the multiplicative operator "*" and its operands being grouped together at a lower level of the parse tree, giving them higher priority than the "+" operator and its operands, thus removing any ambiguity from the grammar. So all three statements are true, and the correct answer is (C).

7. **C**

Any time a sequential search is performed, whether it is on an array, a list, or any other data structure that can be searched sequentially from beginning to end, the maximum possible number of searches is the number of items stored in the data structure. Concerning the array in this question there are 500 items (integers) stored. For a binary search, the maximum possible number of searches is always the lowest power of two that exceeds the number of items, which in this case is 9, because 2 raised to the 9th power is 512. So the answer has to be (C).

8. **D**

The call to function *f* passes a reference to *j* in the form of the parameter *i*, but, although *j* is referenced, it is not changed. The second statement in *f* assigns the value *0* to *i*, and simultaneously to *j*, but they were already *0*. Thus, the only variable changed in *f* is *k*, which is assigned the value *3* in the third statement, and, by the scope of rules of C, is the same as the *k* declared in the calling function, *main.* So,

$$j + k = 0 + 3 = 3$$

and the answer is (D).

9. **E**

First-come-first-serve (FCFS) serves all processes in the order they arrive, or are queued, which may not be fair to short jobs that have to wait a long time for the longer jobs to be completed, but no process is ever deprived of a chance to run. The practice of *aging* will always eventually increase the priority of a process until it is executed. Also, operating systems that dispatch processes by the round-robin system of dispatching (each process in turn is given a time slice) will consistently prevent starvation. Since all three are true, the correct answer is (E).

10. **D**

Statement I is true. If one examines how an AND gate is formed by using strictly NOR gates, or an OR gate is by using strictly NAND gates, it becomes obvious that designs limited to only one type of gate are much more complicated.

(a)

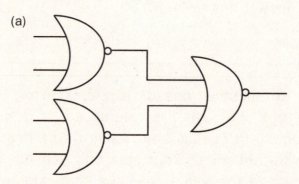

(b)

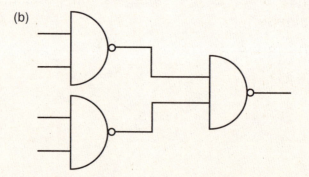

Statement II is also true—the same principle as I applies, except the components are represented by Boolean expressions.

$$\neg[\neg(A + A) + \neg(B + B)]$$

(a)

$$\neg[\neg(A \cdot A) + \neg(B \cdot B)]$$

(b)

Karnaugh maps are useful tools, so III doesn't make any sense, therefore, the correct answer is (D), I and II only.

11. **A**

Statement I is obviously true. The first element of the list is pointed to by *P1*, so it can be found immediately. And also, unlinking the first item of a list takes the same amount of time, whether the length is two, or a thousand. Statement II is a little more tricky. Regarding statement II, if a linked list is quite long, and the search begins at the the first element, then it will take a significant amount of time to find the second to last item. However, if the search begins at the last element (pointed to by *P2*) then the second to last item will be found almost immediately. Statement II says "required time," not "possible time," so it is a true statement. Statement III is false, because deleting an item from a doubly linked list involves reassigning four pointers, rather than just two. Thus, the answer is (A), I and II only.

12. **C**

The input 1011101 is accepted and produces the output 1110110, as shown below, so (A) and (B) are both true statements.

State	Input	Transition State	Output
1	1	1	1
1	0	2	1
2	1	3	1
3	1	2	0
2	1	3	1
3	0	4	1
4	1	5	0
5	—	—	—

The inputs 00101 and 10101 are both accepted, as shown, so (E) is true. Also, both these inputs result in an ouput of 11110, which proves (D). However, it is easy to see by examining the automaton that any input that ends in 101, and is in State 1, or State 3, just prior to the last three inputs, will not be accepted. So (C) is the only answer choice that does not make a true statement, and therefore is the correct answer.

State	Input	Transition State	Output	State	Input	Transition State	Output
1	0	2	1	1	1	1	1
2	0	2	1	1	0	2	1
2	1	3	1	2	1	3	1
3	0	4	1	3	0	4	1
4	1	5	0	4	1	5	0
5	—	—	—	5	—	—	—

13. (C)

We can quickly eliminate three possibilities—this is because the only production that derives 0 is: $B \longrightarrow 00A$. And answers (A), (B), and (D) all have at least one 0, but none have consecutive 0s. Answer (D) is ludicrous, because the only production that terminates is $A \longrightarrow 1$, but answer (D) consists strickly of 0s. This leaves (C), which can be derived as follows

$$S ==> AB ==> A00A ==> 100A ==> 1001.$$

So (C) is the correct answer.

14. **A**

Consider the excitation equation for the *JK* flip-flop,

$$\vec{Q} = \overline{JQ} + \overline{KQ}.$$

If we substitute 1 for both *J and K,* we get

$$\vec{Q} = \overline{1 \wedge Q} + \overline{1 \wedge Q}$$ which simplifies to

$$= \overline{Q}$$

and 0 ANDed with anything is 0, so we get

$$= 1 \wedge \overline{Q} + 0$$ then by the Idempotent Law for OR we get

$$= 1 \wedge \overline{Q}$$ next, the Idempotent Law for AND derives

$$= \overline{Q}$$

So *J* = 1, *K* = 1 causes *Q* to toggle, and (A) is the correct answer.

15. **A**

Statement I is true by the definition of *O(f(n))*. We say the constants *M* and *C* testify to the big-O relationship between *T(n)* and *f(n)*. Statement II is obviously false. This is because some computers are more powerful than others, although the big-O relationship still holds with a different constant *C*. Statement III is essentially the fallacy contained in II, in reverse. We must pick constants *M* and *C* once and for all (on a specific computer), or they fit the definition of variables, not constants. And more importantly, we haven't learned anything by performing the running time analysis.

16. **D**

The definition of a rooted tree consists of three parts: 1) there must be a unique node, called the root, that has no predecessor, 2) every node other than the root must have only one predecessor, and 3) there must be a unique path from the root to every other node. The tree in this problem can be seen to fit this definition by inspection, so

(A) is true. None of the nodes have more than two branches; therefore the tree is binary, and (B) is true. The height of a node is the longest path to any leaf node. The height of a tree is the height of the root node, which in this case is 2. This means (C) is true. (E) is also true, because any binary tree can be traversed in either postorder or preorder. However, even though all of the successors of each node are in order from left to right, a binary search would not find G, because it wouldn't look to the right of the root node, R. Thus, the answer is (D), because the tree is **NOT** searchable by a binary search.

17. **C**

In this example, Fibonacci numbers for the first two integers, *0* and *1*, are not computed recursively, but, if they get past an **if** test (see code for function *fibo*), they are simply returned. However, succeeding integers are computed recursively, as presented in the table below, with the value returned being *fibo (n–1) + fibo (n–2)*. As shown, the value returned for $n = 7$ is *13*, which means the correct answer is (C).

n	fibo (n)	fibo (n–1)	fibo (n–2)	fibo (n–1) + fibo (n–2)
0	0	—	—	—
1	1	—	—	—
2	1	1	0	1
3	2	1	1	2
4	3	2	1	3
5	5	3	2	5
6	8	5	3	8
7	13	8	5	13

18. **E**

This question is deceptively simple because the solution of the recurrence relation is not asked for, just the recurrence relation that would be set up, that if solved, would provide an expression for the running time in terms of constants *a* (the time to execute the first two statements of *fibo)* and *b* (the time to execute the first and third statements of *fibo).* The time *T(n)* for $n \geq 2$ is the sum of *b* (the first and third statements are executed anytime *n* is *2* or greater) and the time for the two recursive calls in the fourth line: $T(n-1)$ and $T(n-2)$. So the recurrence relation is

$$T(n) = a \qquad\qquad\qquad for\ n < 2$$

$$T(n) = b + T(n-1) + T(n-2) \qquad for\ n \leq 2$$

and the answer is (E).

19. **C**

Top-down programming is a generalized approach for organizing a program. For example, a payroll program may be represented at its highest level by a square labeled PAYROLL, that in turn is connected to three smaller squares, that represent the next highest level, labled: INPUT PAYROLL DATA, COMPUTE PAYROLL DATA, and OUTPUT PAYROLL DATA. Each square (representing a module) is broken down into smaller and smaller modules until writing actual code is the next logical step. *Divide and conquer* programming pertains more to specific programming tasks than top-down, but it is similar to, and part of, the top-down approach. Since both of these philosophies are far more generalized than breaking down a single function into separate parts for each parameter, both (A) and (B) are wrong choices. The *water fall model* pertains to the overall software development process, beginning with the requirements definition and ending with long-term software maintenance. *Software engineering* is an overall discipline that includes software documentation, design, and development. Since neither of these two terms deal specifically with a function, (D) and (E) are definitely wrong choices. However, *shilling* is by definition the process of breaking down a function into component parts that only accept one parameter. Thus, the correct answer is (C).

20. **B**

This question is tricky in two ways. First, due to the way the **if-else** construct works, when the **if** test is passed, the **else** branch doesn't execute. This means that, although the **else** test would be true when *i* = *30,* that test is not made—because when *i* = *30,* the **if** branch is executed. Another thing that is tricky is that the **if** branch adds *1* to *sum* each time it is executed, while the **else** branch adds the value of *i*. Thus, the **if** branch increments *sum* five times, when *i* **mod** $10 = 0$. And the **else** branch adds 15 and 45 to *sum* one time each, when *i* **mod** $15 = 0$ and *i* **mod** $10 \neq 0$. Therefore,

$$sum = 0 + 5 + 15 + 45 = 65,$$

and the answer is (B).

21. **B**

If the circuit in this problem is divided into three levels: 1) the OR gate and the XOR gate, 2) the NAND gate, and 3) the AND gate, then we can easily reconstruct the Boolean representation, as follows:

Level 1. $A \vee B$ $B + C$

Level 2. $((A \vee B) \; {}^\wedge A)$ $B + C$

Level 3. $(((A \vee B) {}^\wedge A)) {}^\wedge (B + C)$

Next, we can apply DeMorgan's Law to the output of the NAND gate,

$$((A \vee B) {}^\wedge A) = \overline{(A \vee B)} \vee \overline{A}$$

and then apply DeMorgan's Law to the output of the OR gate,

$$\overline{(A \vee B)} \vee \overline{A} = \overline{A} {}^\wedge \overline{B} \vee \overline{A} = \overline{AB} \vee \overline{A}$$

then substitute the simplified output of NAND gate back into 3. to get

$$(((A \vee B) {}^\wedge A)) {}^\wedge (B + C) = (\overline{AB} \vee \overline{A}) {}^\wedge (B + C)$$

which means the answer is (B).

22. **A**

The concept of context-free grammars was indeed originated by N. Chomsky, but for human languages, not computer languages, so (B) is wrong. A good definition of a context-free grammar is one that can be defined by Backus-Naur Form rules, so (C) is obviously not correct. As for (D), despite his important contribution to computer science, Alan Turing had nothing to do with context-free grammars. Also, the chief advantage of context-free grammars is the richness of functionality allowed languages defined in this way, so (E) is also incorrect. The statement in (A) homes in on the difference between a context-sensitive and a context-free grammar; therefore, (A) is the correct choice.

23. **B**

Since 50 percent of a program won't benefit from additional processors, the first 180 seconds is a given; however, if there are three processors the total time can still be reduced substantially:

180 seconds + (180 seconds/3) = 240 seconds for three processors,

and if there are five processors, the total time can be reduced even further:

180 seconds + (180 seconds/5) = 216 seconds for five processors.

This indicates that (B) is the correct answer.

24. **C**

This problem is straightforward. By the table of minterms

$$m^3 = \overline{A}\,BC, \qquad m^4 = A\overline{B}\,\overline{C}, \quad m^5 = A\overline{B}\,C$$

so

$$f(A,\ B,\ C) = m^3 + m^4 + m^5 = \overline{A}\,BC + A\overline{B}\,\overline{C} + A\overline{B}\,C$$

and (C) is the correct answer.

25. **D**

The union operator creates a set of strings comprised of all the elements of either of its two operands (regular expressions denoting sets of strings). The union operator is associative and has lower precedence than concatenation, so it is possible to form the union of several sets without parentheses. However, parentheses are required if the union is being concatenated, or being worked on by the closure operator. (A), (B), and (E) are wrong answers, because they can conceivably begin with a digit. (C) is also incorrect, because there is no way a word formed from (C) could have more than two digits. (D), by the definition of concatenation, must begin with a letter, and, by the definition of both union and closure, is followed by zero or more pairs of letters and digits in any length or combination. (D) represents all odd-length alphanumeric words beginning with a letter, and is, therefore, the correct answer.

26. **C** ──

If dynamic scoping is in effect, the variables *i* and *j* in **procedure** *A* will be associated with the *i* and *j* of calling **procedure** *B*, so *j* will be *4* when *A* returns. When *B* returns to the main program *j* will not be affected by what happened to locally declared *j* in procedure *B*, so *j* will be equal to *35*. If static scoping is used, *i* and *j* in **procedure** *A* will be linked at compile time to the most immediate enclosing program or subprogram, which, in this case, is the main program. So, in **procedure** *A*, the *j* of the main program will be doubled to *70*, and the value of the locally declared *j* in **procedure** *B* will be irrelevant to the main program. Thus, the answer is (C) dynamic: 35, static: 70.

27. **A** ──

The trouble with (B) and (C) is that they only change the value of pointer *X*, and do nothing to change the value of the *nextPtr* field of the cell *X* is pointing to. (D) and (E) would result in compile-time errors, because *cellPtr* is a type, not a variable. However, (A) changes *nextPtr* of the cell previous to the one to be deleted, and does it in such a way that it points to the first cell beyond the one to be deleted. This effectively deletes the cell from the list, so the correct answer is (A).

28. **A**

The four AND gates are in parallel, so the delay is the same as the delay for one. By the same token, the two inverters are in parallel, so the delay for them is the same as one inverter. There is, however, no way the delay can be less than the sum of the delay for one AND gate (20 ns) and one inverter (12 ns), because they are in series. So the delay is 20 ns plus 12 ns, or 32 ns, and (A) is the correct answer.

29. **B**

This question starts where the previous one left off: the delay of 32 ns to decode the address lines. To that must be added the delay before the bit stored in the memory is output through the AND gate from the time it has been enabled by the SELECT line. This is an additional 20 ns, so the answer is (B) 52 ns.

30. **B**

This question also starts where question 28 left off: the delay of 32 ns to decode the address lines. Because there is an input to the memory cell, the delay of the two parallel AND gates, which allow input (20 ns) to the RS flip-flop, must be added to the delay of the decoder. (The two inverters would not cause a delay because DATA-IN and READ/WRITE assume their values at the same time as the address A^n.) We can ignore the delay of the AND gate at the output of the memory cell, because that has nothing to do with a write. So the answer is computed as follows: 32 ns (to decode the address) plus 20 ns (for the two AND gates) plus 20 ns to account for the transition time of the RS flip-flop, or (B) 72 ns.

31. **E**

TCP/IP uses whatever protocol is being used on the current network to transmit IP packets across the next hop; it could be almost any protocol. This layer is also sometimes called the Interface Layers;

regardless, it could be many different protocols, so the answer is (E), all of the above.

32. **C**

Once a decimal number has been converted to binary, the task of converting to hexadecimal is greatly simplified. The best way to accomplish this is to group the bits into units of four and write their hexadecimal equivalents underneath.

1	0001	1100	0000	0000	1110	1011	0111	0001
1	1	C	1	0	E	B	7	1

This makes it obvious that the answer is (C).

33. **B**

The statement made in I is a true statement: the page fault handler and the I/O supervisor are not synchronized—but they don't need to be. This is not a reader/writer situation where one process is supplying information for the other; instead, the two concurrent procedures are simply using the same resource, so II is not relevant by the same logic. However, for example, if the page fault handler, or the I/O supervisor, were interrupted in the middle of the queuing operation, the result would be the *end_Q* pointer still points to a process requesting I/O, while the link field (*next*) of the last record in the queue pointing to a process requesting page fault handling. Since each succeeding process requesting I/O or page fault service would also be lost, this would lead to a catastrophic failure of the system. Thus, the answer is (B), III only.

34. **C**

(A) and (D) are wrong for the same reasons described in 33. (B) is wrong because the test and set instruction is positioned exactly at the beginning of the critical section. (E) is also wrong, since it is very important to set the flag at the end of the critical section—so that other processes waiting on *s* may execute their critical section. But (C) is right on target—it is the tying up of a processor resource by looping on the test and set instruction that has caused the operation (originally developed by IBM) not to catch on.

35. **D**

All three of these statements are true. The main idea behind semaphores was to find a way to free the resources of a process blocked on a critical region. The best way to do that is to turn the process over to the operating system immediately following the execution of a **P** operation on a semaphore, so I is true. The operating system will cause a process blocked on a semaphore to run again where it left off, so II is also true. And III is true, because the two concurrent procedures in this question are independent, as explained in 33. Thus, the answer is (D), I, II, and III.

36. **B**

The formula for possible assignments of *k* values to *n* objects is k^n. The first character of the password can be any letter of the alphabet, or the underscore, so that is *27* values. Since there is only one object, the first letter of the password, there are 27^1, or 27 possibilities for the first character. For the remaining 8 characters (or objects), there are 37 possible values: 26 (number of letters of the alphabet) + 1 (for the underscore) + 10 (the number of digits). So that is 37^8, but that must be multiplied by the 27 possible first letter that go with it. This means the answer is $27 * 37^8$, or (B).

37. **C**

The operators, including the assignment operator "=," are all accepted with only one transition. The **while**, **begin**, and **end** keywords are clearly accepted. That leaves **for** and **function,** which are only accepted if the automaton makes the right guess when it sees an f.

This means that the automaton is not deterministic; however, it does accept both **for** and **function.** So, the correct answer is (C).

38. **B**

The automaton is non-deterministic in the case of **for**, because it must guess whether an f input is the first character of **for**, or the first character of **function**, so (A) is wrong. However, in the case of **while** and **begin**, it is deterministic, because it accepts them without having to guess, so (C) and (E) are also incorrect statements. (D) is false, because the main advantage of automata is that they are easily convertible to code. That leaves (B) as the only answer that makes sense, because any nondeterministic automaton can be converted to a deterministic automaton.

39. **C**

The nature of computer multiplication is that it is (even with multipliers on board) basically repeated addition. However, vector processors have pipelines that allow a number of multipliers and multiplicands to be at various stages of the multiplicative process. In the case of multiplying two matrices, a continuous computational flow is made possible, resulting in an extremely fast and efficient operation. So I is a true statement. Statement III is also true, because without components that can be multiplied in parallel, the pipeline can't work. Statement II is incorrect, because a vector processor is a digital device. And statement IV is not worth considering, since disregarding the sign bit only results in erroneous computations. Therefore, the answer is (C) I and III only.

40. **C**

The CRC is computed from the message polynomial *G(x)* and the generating polynomial *P(x)*. First *G(x)* is multiplied by the highest term in the generator polynomial *P(x)*. Then *G(x)* is divided by *P(x)*, except the subtraction sub-operation is replaced with an XOR. The remainder, 10001, is the CRC, so the correct answer is (C).

$$
\begin{array}{r}
111110101 \\
110101\overline{)10011111000000} \\
110101 \\
\hline
100101 \\
110101 \\
\hline
100001 \\
110101 \\
\hline
101000 \\
110101 \\
\hline
111010 \\
110101 \\
\hline
011110 \\
110101 \\
\hline
101011 \\
110101
\end{array} = 11110 \text{ or CRC}
$$

41. **D**

Although switching speeds vary from one implementation to another, on balance CMOS remains slightly slower than its rival technologies—especially ECL. This means (A) is not correct. Answer (B) is also wrong, because all semiconductor technologies require doping with both p- and n-material. (C) is ludicrous, because without transistors we'd be back to the days when computers occupied entire rooms. The trouble with (E) is that CMOS by definition is more complicated than either P-MOS or N-MOS, because it is a combination of both. That leaves (D), which is a true statement since, by placing P-MOS and N-MOS devices adjacent to each other on a chip, the current flow is reduced to almost zero—which is the biggest asset of CMOS. So, the correct answer is (D).

42. **A**

Answers (B) through (D) simply reverse the characteristics of dynamic and static RAM. It is the data in *static* RAM that is not lost when the power is turned off. *Dynamic* RAM looses its data. Also, it is static RAM that has much shorter access times compared to dynamic RAM. And, it is dynamic RAM that loses data on every read, requiring that it immediately be written back. So (B) through (D) are incorrect. In answer choice (E), the requirement that dynamic RAM be refreshed periodically is a liability (not an asset), because it takes up processor time, and detracts from system stability. However, dynamic RAM is much less expensive. This, of course, has been a strong incentive for engineers to find a way to work with it. So, the answer is (A).

43. **C** ───

In order for the contents of register R^3 be transferred to register R^4, they must first be transferred onto the bus, which happens when R^3 is selected by the multiplexer (MUX). The MUX selects R^3 when its inputs are 10 (see table). Once the contents of R^3 are transferred onto the bus, they are decoded to register R^4, if the decoder's inputs are 00 (also, see table); so the answer is (C).

44. **A** ───

The first micro-operation executed following the interrupt is as follows:

i. C^2T^0:   PC <— I_adr.   Program counter gets interrupt address

It should have been something like this (assuming an on-board stack pointer: SP).

C^2T^0: MAR <— SP   MAR gets stack pointer (SP)

C^2T^1: M [MAR] <— MBR   Save instruction on stack

C^2T^2: MBR <— PC   MBR get program counter

C^2T^3: M [MAR] <— MBR   Save program counter (PC) on stack

C^2T^4: PC <— I_adr.   Program counter gets interrupt address

In order for the interrupted program to resume execution following the interrupt service, the instruction must be saved. Since the interrupt followed the fetch cycle, the execute cycle has yet to be preferred for the instruction that was just fetched. In addition, it is very important to save the PC, otherwise the address of the macro program in RAM will be lost.

Control units (CU) for more complex CPUs will save many more registers either automatically, or by allowing the assembly programmer to decide which registers to save. The above is the minimum required.

Micro-operation I overwrites the program counter immediately, making it impossible for the currently executing program to resume later. So the correct answer is (A), I.

45. **D**

First the ASCII values of A and 1 are XORed as follows:

01001010 XOR 00110001= 01111011

$$= 64 + 32 + 16 + 8 + 2 + 1$$

$$= 123$$

123 is then divided by the modulus 10, leaving the remainder 3. But slot 3 is already occupied, so the result of the hash is rehashed by multiplying it by 2, and dividing it again by the modulus 10, which leaves the remainder 6. However, slot 6 is also occupied, so the result is rehashed again, yielding a 9 as the result, which is an open slot. Therefore, the answer is (D).

46. **D**

If we add the **page register** to the **page table register** we get 411 as the address in the page table holding information about page 11. The flag's setting to 1 indicates the page is currently in memory, and the 17 indicates it is stored in page frame 17. Next, we multiply 17 times the number of words in a page, 1024, and add that result to the address of the first page frame, 2000, to get the beginning address of the page frame,

$$17 * 1024 + 2000 = 19408$$

Next, we add the index within that page, contained in the **index register**:

$$19408 + 312 = 19720$$

So the answer is (D).

47. **B**

The way to begin the conversion of the infix expression to prefix is to first set off any pair of operands and their associated operator, as shown below.

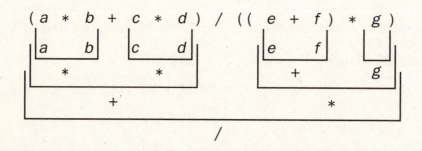

Next, the figure should be scanned from the left until an operator is picked up, then that operator should be written down. The process should keep repeating itself at higher levels, until an atomic pair of operands is found. The results of the first four left-to-right scans are as follows:

/

/+

/+*

/+*ab

When a pair of atomic operands is found, the scanning process should begin again at the highest level at which an operator (or single

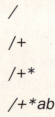

operand, in some cases) hasn't been picked up. The results of the next two scans are shown below:

/+*ab*

/+ab*cd

Another pair of atomic operands were found. The process should repeat until the entire infix expression has been accounted for. The results of the next four scans are shown below:

/+*ab*cd*

/+*ab*cd*+

/+*ab*cd*+ef

/+*ab*cd*+efg

Therefore, the answer is (B).

48. **A**

It has been proven that if the sequence of resource requests that a process will make is known, deadlock can be avoided, which makes statement I true. Along the same lines, if the sequence of resource requests is not known, but the maximum resource requirements of a process are, an algorithm known as the Banker's Algorithm can be used to avoid deadlock, although the use of resources will be less efficient. Therefore, statement III is true. However, the second statement regarding a *hierarchical allocation* of resources pertains to the policy of deadlock prevention, *not* avoidance. So, only statements I and III are true (with respect to avoidance), and the answer is (A).

49. **C**

The purpose of **P** and **V** operations is to eliminate wasteful looping by blocked processes, so (B) is wrong. In answer choice (D), there is only one producer and one consumer. However, the **P** and **V** operations provide functionality similar to the WAIT and SIGNAL operations, yielding a synchronization between processes, which shows that (C) is correct and that (A) should be eliminated. Therefore, the correct answer is (C).

50. **B**

When the *block chain* method is used, the file descriptor can optionally be kept in only one block with the other blocks containing a pointer to the block with the descriptor. So (A) is not a true statement. Note that most file systems organize free disk space into large blocks, which are more manageable than one contiguous chain. But a *block chain* file does not need to be limited to the original block of free space from which it was created. This means (C) is also untrue. When the *file map* method is used, access times are slower than those of the *index* method, but are still much faster than those of the *block chain* method, which are prohibitively slow for individual records. Therefore, (D) is incorrect. Most file management systems prefer to use the same block size for the entire file system, and (E) describes the opposite of this reality and thus can be eliminated. One of the disadvantages for the faster access of the *index* method is that of greater complexity, especially when one considers scenarios that involve the file index outgrowing a single block. So, (B) is the right answer.

51. **C**

The address where the A register will be stored in RAM is contained in the last 12 bits of the STA instruction. In this example, that address is binary 101101110010. It can be converted to decimal form in the following way:

1	2048
0	
1	512
1	256
0	
1	64
1	32
1	16
0	
0	
1	2
0	
	____
	2930

which means the answer is (C).

52. **E**

The address where the A register will be stored in RAM is obtained by adding the last 12 bits of the STAX instruction to the contents of the X register, as follows:

Address field of STAX instruction	101101110010
Contents of X register	0001101101110010
	0010011011100100

The result can be converted to decimal in the following way:

```
0
1        8192
0
0
1        1024
1         512
0
1         128
1          64
1          32
0
0
1           4
0
0        _____
         9956
```

So the answer is (E) 9,956.

53. **D**

Vectors can be represented in multi-dimensional space with or without the dot product, so (A) doesn't make any sense. Furthermore, the dot product bear no relevance to Gauss-Jordan elimination, so (B) is wrong. Answer (C) is close, because the dot product is proportional to the product of the lengths of two vectors, multiplied by the cosine of their common angle. But a vector is not a reliable measure of length, and this does not exactly answer the question, because it does not address why it is called a scalar; therefore, (C) is not correct. However, a scalar is a number that, unlike a vector, has no direction, which means the definition of a dot product in answer choice (D) was right on target. Therefore, (D) is the correct answer.

54. A ————————————————————————————————————

Coaxial cable is actually less flexible than unshielded twisted pairs, which means that (B) is incorrect. As for (C), coax is capable of broadband transmission, but so are other cables. So, (C) is not the right answer. And just like other forms of cabling, coax requires repeaters; therefore, (D) can be eliminated. The popularity of ADSL doesn't affect coaxial cable, because ADSL is used strictly with twisted pair. That brings us back to the first choice, which accurately describes the reason for the continued high demand for coax: it is virtually immune to low and moderate levels of background noise and electromagnetic interference. Therefore, the correct answer is (A).

55. E ————————————————————————————————————

If we rearrange the original formula slightly, we get

AMAT = hit time + (miss rate * access time) +
   (miss rate * (block size/transfer rate))

Then, if we substitute numbers (with cc representing clock cycles),

$$AMAT = 4\ cc + \left[\frac{1024\ b}{128\ Bb} \times 4\ cc\right] + \left[\frac{1024\ b}{128\ Bb} \times \frac{Bb}{2\frac{b}{cc}}\right]$$

$$= 4\ cc + \frac{32\ cc}{B} + 4\ cc$$

$$= 8\ cc + \frac{32\ cc}{B}$$

We soon realize that the only term whose value changes with block size (B) is the one in the middle, miss rate * access time, or

32/B,   in this case.

Also, we can easily compute all possible values for the middle term, as follows:

miss rate * access time =

32/b	B
1	32
1/2	64
1/4	128
1/8	256
1/16	512

If we substitute in the smallest result, we get

AMAT = 4 cc + 1/16 cc + 4 cc

= 8 1/16

for a block size of 512 bytes.

Thus, it is clear the correct answer is (E) 512 bytes.

56. D

It wouldn't be practical for a fixed-sized stack record to hold the individual cells of a linked list that theoretically could grow to any size. The same concept applies in the case of a dynamic array, so both (A) and (B) are wrong. Global variables in C language are static and not relevant to a dynamically changing activation stack, which eliminates (C). In the case of (E), the stack pointer would have to be separate from the stack in order to point to it. (D) is the only remaining option, and since an activation record is both an efficient and convenient place to hold a pointer to the next lower record on the stack (the *previous* activation record), it is the right answer.

57. **(A)**

A directory tree structure is not only user friendly (easily comprehensible by humans) it is what is in common use by the user interface, either in command line or graphical UI. This phenomenon makes the translation from the internal file structure to the external one much easier, because they are both trees. Therefore, I is a true statement. By the definition of a rooted tree, every path from the root to a leaf (a file) is unique; it is just a question of combining the directory and file names (usually with a forward or backward slash in between) to come up with globally uniques names. This means II is true. The biggest disadvantage of trees is that they are inherently nonsequential, often requiring hours to defragment. So III is the opposite of this reality. Thus, (A), I and II only, is correct.

58. **(A)**

First, we convert the following infix expression to postfix.

(a * b + c * d) / ((e + f) * g)

Now, set off any pair of operands and their associated operator, as shown below.

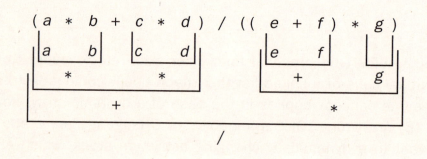

Next, the above figure is scanned in the same way as it was in Question 47, except you begin from the right, instead of from the left, yielding:

ab*cd*+ef+g*/

Then, we scan from left to right pushing each operand onto the stack:

>   *PUSH (a), PUSH (b)*

Then, when an operator, *, is scanned, the operands are removed,

>   *POP, POP*

and the operation is performed, $a * b = 2$. Then, the result is pushed onto the stack:

>   *PUSH (2)*

Next, the scan continues, pushing two more operands

>   PUSH (*c*), PUSH (*d*)

Then, the operator, *, is scanned, so its operators are removed,

>   *POP, POP*

and the operation is performed, $c * d = 70$, and the result is pushed onto the stack:

>   *PUSH (70)*

These stack operations matched those in answer (A), so that is the correct answer.

59. **E**

The first two graphs are obviously planar, because none of the edges intersect. The third graph appears at first to be nonplanar, but it can be redrawn as planar, as shown below:

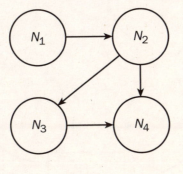

or

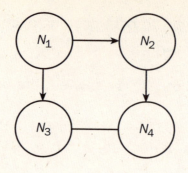

This means that the first three graphs are planar, thus eliminating choices (A)–(D). However, the fourth graph is one of the simpler non-planar graphs that is known as K3,3 in connection with a famous theorem by Kuratowski. Since IV is nonplanar, the answer is (E).

60. D

All three statements (I–III) are valid descriptions of the three parts of a 64-bit socket address that are used for system calls on a client server network. This means the correct answer is (D).

61. E

As shown in the figure below, all that is necessary to alleviate the cycle that creates deadlock is to remove edges 1 and 7. So the correct answer is (E).

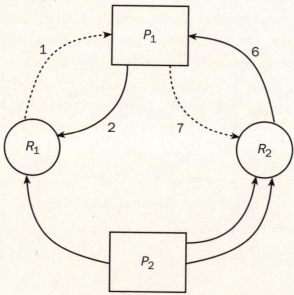

62. **D**

Answers (A), (B), (C), and (E) are all correct in an intuitive sense. The function *MergeNbrList* does merge a list of items—see answer (A)—that is the name of the field whose value determines the order of the list. And the items are numbers—see answer (B)—and, not only that, but they are integer numbers—see answer (C). Also, answer (E) could be considered correct, because these integer/number/items are stored in a linked list of records (technically **struct** in C language). But (D) covers all of the bases, and is technically more rigorous, which makes it the best answer.

63. **A**

Nodes is a pointer to a node that can be used to access the identifier of the graph, but it doesn't identify the node, so II can be eliminated. The array *Graph* consists of all the nodes of the graph, and *index* really does identify individual nodes, but III is *Graph [index]* not *index*, so III can also be eliminated. That leaves I *NodeName*, which is an integer variable that identifies an individual graph node. This means the correct answer is (A).

64. **C**

Although *depth* doesn't return a value, it is working with global variables *index* and *g*, so it is able to add to the information stored in the graph, which means (A) is not the answer. (B) is also wrong, because *depth* visits *every* node of *g*, it just doesn't necessarily find every path to every node. Since there is no attempt to compute the depth of the nodes, (D) is not a true statement. The correct choice is (C), because a depth-first search does indeed create a tree of nodes, but not one that necessarily identifies every arc between the nodes.

65. **E**

This is a much more straightforward question than first appearances would indicate, because the recursive calls don't have to be accounted for. All one has to do is carefully examine the code for *depthFrst,* and it becomes clear that each node is visited no more than once for each value of index. If one of the recursive calls that are made by *depth* have already visited a node, then it has been marked; therefore, it is not visited the second time around by *depth.* Therefore, the correct answer is (E) $T(n) = O(n)$.

66. (D)

Statement IV includes three positive propositional literals: p^1, p^2, *and q.* Since a Horn clause, by definition, can include at most one positive propositional literal, statement IV is not correct. Statements I and III include only one positive propositional literal, *q,* so they are correct, and statement II includes only negative propostional literals, so it is correct as well. Therefore, the right answer is (D), I, II, and III.

67. (C)

Consider the following sequence of queue states:

enqueue (I)	C, B, F, G, I
enqueue (A)	C, B, F, G, I, A
dequeue	B, F, G, I, A
enqueue (D)	B, F, G, I, A, D
enqueue (H)	B, F, G, I, A, D, H
dequeue	F, G, I, A, D, H

Since the final state is consistent with the question, and the sequence of operations match answer (C) exactly, it is the correct answer.

68. **E**

While examining the automaton, we can see that although there are many possible paths, the set of strings it accepts is very simple: *a* followed by one or more *b*'s, followed by a *c*. So (E) is the answer.

69. **B**

If we count the original trie, there are 16 nodes. "Wherefore" adds 5, including the *; "whether" adds 5, including the *; and "house" adds 4, including the *. That brings the total to 30.

70. **E**

The relation defined by two numbers having the same remainder or modulus is actually one of the better known equivalence relations, which means it has all three properties: reflexitivity, symmetry, and transitivity. This means the answer is (E), I, II, and III.

Answer Sheet

Answer Sheet

1. Ⓐ Ⓑ Ⓒ Ⓓ Ⓔ		36. Ⓐ Ⓑ Ⓒ Ⓓ Ⓔ	
2. Ⓐ Ⓑ Ⓒ Ⓓ Ⓔ		37. Ⓐ Ⓑ Ⓒ Ⓓ Ⓔ	
3. Ⓐ Ⓑ Ⓒ Ⓓ Ⓔ		38. Ⓐ Ⓑ Ⓒ Ⓓ Ⓔ	
4. Ⓐ Ⓑ Ⓒ Ⓓ Ⓔ		39. Ⓐ Ⓑ Ⓒ Ⓓ Ⓔ	
5. Ⓐ Ⓑ Ⓒ Ⓓ Ⓔ		40. Ⓐ Ⓑ Ⓒ Ⓓ Ⓔ	
6. Ⓐ Ⓑ Ⓒ Ⓓ Ⓔ		41. Ⓐ Ⓑ Ⓒ Ⓓ Ⓔ	
7. Ⓐ Ⓑ Ⓒ Ⓓ Ⓔ		42. Ⓐ Ⓑ Ⓒ Ⓓ Ⓔ	
8. Ⓐ Ⓑ Ⓒ Ⓓ Ⓔ		43. Ⓐ Ⓑ Ⓒ Ⓓ Ⓔ	
9. Ⓐ Ⓑ Ⓒ Ⓓ Ⓔ		44. Ⓐ Ⓑ Ⓒ Ⓓ Ⓔ	
10. Ⓐ Ⓑ Ⓒ Ⓓ Ⓔ		45. Ⓐ Ⓑ Ⓒ Ⓓ Ⓔ	
11. Ⓐ Ⓑ Ⓒ Ⓓ Ⓔ		46. Ⓐ Ⓑ Ⓒ Ⓓ Ⓔ	
12. Ⓐ Ⓑ Ⓒ Ⓓ Ⓔ		47. Ⓐ Ⓑ Ⓒ Ⓓ Ⓔ	
13. Ⓐ Ⓑ Ⓒ Ⓓ Ⓔ		48. Ⓐ Ⓑ Ⓒ Ⓓ Ⓔ	
14. Ⓐ Ⓑ Ⓒ Ⓓ Ⓔ		49. Ⓐ Ⓑ Ⓒ Ⓓ Ⓔ	
15. Ⓐ Ⓑ Ⓒ Ⓓ Ⓔ		50. Ⓐ Ⓑ Ⓒ Ⓓ Ⓔ	
16. Ⓐ Ⓑ Ⓒ Ⓓ Ⓔ		51. Ⓐ Ⓑ Ⓒ Ⓓ Ⓔ	
17. Ⓐ Ⓑ Ⓒ Ⓓ Ⓔ		52. Ⓐ Ⓑ Ⓒ Ⓓ Ⓔ	
18. Ⓐ Ⓑ Ⓒ Ⓓ Ⓔ		53. Ⓐ Ⓑ Ⓒ Ⓓ Ⓔ	
19. Ⓐ Ⓑ Ⓒ Ⓓ Ⓔ		54. Ⓐ Ⓑ Ⓒ Ⓓ Ⓔ	
20. Ⓐ Ⓑ Ⓒ Ⓓ Ⓔ		55. Ⓐ Ⓑ Ⓒ Ⓓ Ⓔ	
21. Ⓐ Ⓑ Ⓒ Ⓓ Ⓔ		56. Ⓐ Ⓑ Ⓒ Ⓓ Ⓔ	
22. Ⓐ Ⓑ Ⓒ Ⓓ Ⓔ		57. Ⓐ Ⓑ Ⓒ Ⓓ Ⓔ	
23. Ⓐ Ⓑ Ⓒ Ⓓ Ⓔ		58. Ⓐ Ⓑ Ⓒ Ⓓ Ⓔ	
24. Ⓐ Ⓑ Ⓒ Ⓓ Ⓔ		59. Ⓐ Ⓑ Ⓒ Ⓓ Ⓔ	
25. Ⓐ Ⓑ Ⓒ Ⓓ Ⓔ		60. Ⓐ Ⓑ Ⓒ Ⓓ Ⓔ	
26. Ⓐ Ⓑ Ⓒ Ⓓ Ⓔ		61. Ⓐ Ⓑ Ⓒ Ⓓ Ⓔ	
27. Ⓐ Ⓑ Ⓒ Ⓓ Ⓔ		62. Ⓐ Ⓑ Ⓒ Ⓓ Ⓔ	
28. Ⓐ Ⓑ Ⓒ Ⓓ Ⓔ		63. Ⓐ Ⓑ Ⓒ Ⓓ Ⓔ	
29. Ⓐ Ⓑ Ⓒ Ⓓ Ⓔ		64. Ⓐ Ⓑ Ⓒ Ⓓ Ⓔ	
30. Ⓐ Ⓑ Ⓒ Ⓓ Ⓔ		65. Ⓐ Ⓑ Ⓒ Ⓓ Ⓔ	
31. Ⓐ Ⓑ Ⓒ Ⓓ Ⓔ		66. Ⓐ Ⓑ Ⓒ Ⓓ Ⓔ	
32. Ⓐ Ⓑ Ⓒ Ⓓ Ⓔ		67. Ⓐ Ⓑ Ⓒ Ⓓ Ⓔ	
33. Ⓐ Ⓑ Ⓒ Ⓓ Ⓔ		68. Ⓐ Ⓑ Ⓒ Ⓓ Ⓔ	
34. Ⓐ Ⓑ Ⓒ Ⓓ Ⓔ		69. Ⓐ Ⓑ Ⓒ Ⓓ Ⓔ	
35. Ⓐ Ⓑ Ⓒ Ⓓ Ⓔ		70. Ⓐ Ⓑ Ⓒ Ⓓ Ⓔ	

References

References

Brookshear, J. Glenn. Computer Science: An Overview. 8th ed. Upper Saddle River, N.J.: Addison Wesley, 2004.

Educational Testing Service. GRE: Practicing to Take the Computer Science Test. 3rd ed. 1997.

Lewis, Harry R. and Christos H. Papadimitriou. Elements of Theory of Computation. 2nd ed. Upper Saddle River, N.J.: Prentice Hall, 1997.

Raus, Randall. Essentials of Computer Science I. Piscataway, N.J. Research & Education Association, Inc., 2002.

Raus, Randall. Essentials of Computer Science II. Piscataway, N.J. Research & Education Association, Inc., 1998.

Helpful Websites

Official Website for the GRE: *www.gre.org*

Association for Computing Machinery: *http://portal.acm.org/*

The Free Online Dictionary of Computing: *http://nightflight.com/foldoc*

BABEL, a glossary of computer oriented acronyms and abbreviations: *www.geocities.com/ikind_babel/babel/babel.html*

NIST Dictionary of Algorithms and Data Structures: *www.mist.gov/dads*

Jargon Dictionary: *http://catb.org/~esr/jargon/*